SURVIVING
DIVORCE AND ROOMMATES WITH
PRAYER, MUSIC AND SAILING

BARBARA SHAW

LUMINARE PRESS

WWW.LUMINAREPRESS.COM

Printed in the United States of America

Cover Design: Melissa Lund

Luminare Press
438 Charnelton St., Suite 101
Eugene, OR 97401
www.luminarepress.com

LCCN: 2018947893
ISBN: 978-1-944733-91-9

To my children and grandchildren, with love

CHAPTER ONE

The Office Party: *October 1981*

I didn't know our marriage was in trouble when I picked up the phone to make a call and there was no dial tone. It was late in the evening and I was getting ready to go to bed so I hung up immediately. I thought the phone was off the hook. I picked it up again and the line was silent still.

I asked, "Are you on the line?"

Greg said, "Yes," so I hung up.

I thought our daughter, who just turned two and liked to play with the phone, had picked the phone up and left it off the hook. A few minutes later I heard the front door shut as he left the house. I was pregnant with our second child, and my due date was in a few weeks. I was concerned why he was mysteriously going out without saying anything. He had never done something like that before. I thought maybe he went to the store for cigarettes, but he didn't return until 2:00 a.m. I had locked the bedroom door. I don't know why I did that. I had never done that in the five years we were married. He slept on the couch in the family room. I went downstairs in the morning and he offered no explanation. I could tell he had been drinking and was hung over from the night before. I assumed he went to the golf course to meet with coworkers that were golfing there. I wanted to have an open house after his coworkers played golf at the course up the street, but he said no without an explanation.

I thought he was thinking of me as it might be too close to my delivery date. It seemed odd not to have the group over as we usually had his coworkers to our home when we lived in Southern California. I didn't question his motives, just accepted his feelings. In spite of his late night of drinking he was still planning on driving to pick up my mother. She would be staying with us for the birth of our second child, to help with our daughter when I went to the hospital. I wasn't sure what atmosphere we were bringing my mother into when he drove to pick her up, but I didn't think this was the time to change plans. She had given up her apartment, stored her furniture, and was waiting for him. It was a six-hour drive there and back that same day.

Nothing was said about where he went the night before.

Not long before we left Southern California we attended a Marriage Encounter weekend. I thought no one could go through such a spiritual weekend and not have a lasting relationship. Before he left for work I wrote a letter to him in our notebook from the Marriage Encounter. I left the book on his dresser for him to answer so we could talk about what happened and why. He didn't answer my letter until sometime later.

Birth of Son: *November 1981*

We finally talked and I thought everything was good between us before our son was born. After his birth I felt so blessed, everything was so wonderful. I had so much to be thankful for. A few days later the phone bill came, and when I opened the bill I saw a number that I did not recognize. The amazing thing is that it was the only call out of the area on the phone bill. I realized the call had been placed the night of the golf tournament, the night I picked the phone up and there was no dial tone, so I called the number. I recognized the area code from the other side of San Francisco. A child answered the phone. I tried to find out the name of the person on the phone bill, then a female adult took the phone and spoke. I quickly said, "Is Kathy there?" She said, "No." I knew immediately that she knew who I was. She recognized my voice from when I called my husband at the office. I went upstairs to the bedroom. He was shaving, as we were going out to the park with our children.

I said, "I don't recognize this number on the phone bill, do you?"

He said, "It's the telephone number of a girl at work. I went to her party and had to call for directions."

I became angry and said, "You snuck out and went to a party a few weeks before the birth of our son, knowing that I could have gone into labor at any time, and you didn't even let me know you were going."

He didn't seem to think it was a big deal. He didn't

want to discuss his evening out. Since moving to Walnut Creek I worried about going into labor and how I would get to the hospital as my last two children had been quick births. When my youngest daughter was born we were only a few blocks from the hospital. Since it was early in the morning before he left for work, he was able to drive me to the hospital. When we arrived at the hospital I could feel her coming. The nurse looked under my nightgown and could see we had to hurry. I had been in the hospital less than thirty minutes when she was born. Luckily, I had taken Lamaze classes for natural childbirth and practiced my breathing exercises. I didn't need any medications and the pain was minimal.

It was a few days until Thanksgiving, after the birth of our son, and we were making plans for my daughter and son from my first marriage to join us in Walnut Creek for the holiday. Greg went to pick them up at the airport after work on Wednesday night. When they arrived, my daughter Bett said Greg told her we were not getting along, and were having some problems. She wanted to know what was going on, were we having problems? I wasn't sure myself what was going on, or why he said that to them. I was not aware we were having problems. I was making plans to have our son baptized over the Thanksgiving holiday while both of them were in Walnut Creek. After talking with our Pastor, he suggested waiting a few weeks which would be closer to Christmas. So, I changed the baptism to Christmas when all my family would be together. It wasn't a very happy Thanksgiving after Greg's talk with Bett and FJ. Things were very tense and strained between us. We drove them to the airport, and on the way back I started crying and couldn't stop. On top of just giving birth I was now dealing with whatever problems Greg and I were having. I suggested that maybe we needed to see a marriage counselor, and he agreed. Little did I realize why he agreed to this. I looked through the phone book and made some calls and found someone who would take us during the holiday season. It seemed strange to go to a marriage counselor when we had never had any problems communicating, that was the one thing we always had going for us. We always seemed to be able to talk about anything.

It was during our first session that I asked Greg if he was interested in someone else. His reply was, "What do you mean by interested?"

I found out then that he and the woman from work had started going out to lunch together. She was the one that had the party he had gone to. She had originally asked him to lunch, he said, and then it became more frequent. She was promoted and was not in his office anymore. I recognized her voice when she called late one night and we were in bed. I answered the phone and she said, "Is Kathy there?"

That was the same question I asked when I called her number. When I hung up I said to Greg, "That was your girlfriend."

There was no response from him. If she had called a few minutes earlier I wouldn't have been able to answer, as we were involved like most couples are when in bed.

December 1981

In Southern California I worked as a real estate agent for four years, but I decided to look for a salaried job since the real estate market was down at the time with interest rates at seventeen to eighteen percent. Homes were not selling, and I couldn't pay my expenses while on a commission job any longer. Our expenses were high with our home, and we needed my income. Luckily, we had partners on both of our homes in Southern California. It helped that they were friends, as well as coworkers and partners. They had just moved into our home in Valencia and now were co-owners. Staying home was not easy at this time. I had too much time to dwell on our relationship problems, and my mother was there to help with the kids while I went job hunting. There was a hiring freeze at most government agencies, so I decided to look into jobs in private industry. I went on several interviews but didn't land anything. I stopped by Greg's office while I was out interviewing and was surprised to hear he was out. Everyone was in Sausalito for their Christmas luncheon. I wondered why he didn't say anything, and if he had gone with his former co-worker. We talked several times before he took this promotion to the Bay Area, and how it would affect our lives. We knew the office was a party group. They would leave work and take the "Fun Bus" to Tahoe, gamble and drink all night, and then come back the next morning to work. There had already been several divorces and problems in marriages due to this atmosphere.

BARBARA SHAW

The Christmas Office Party and Christmas Eve

My family was coming to our house for Christmas since we had five bedrooms and plenty of room for everyone. For some reason, Greg stopped getting up on Sundays and going to church with me. We were going to start attending the new members class, but he continued to oversleep. My older son and daughter were flying up from Southern California for Christmas. Greg took the car into the city and said he would pick them up after work, the day before Christmas Eve.

I said, "No, I will pick them up."

I didn't want him to have any more conversations like he had at Thanksgiving. I picked them up at the airport and Greg didn't come home that night. I got up early with Brit and Case, and called his brother. It was early, about 6:30 a.m. I wanted to know if Greg had spent the night with his brother.

"No, he's not here," he said.

We talked for about thirty minutes. He was sure everything would be okay. I called Greg's office at 7:30 a.m.

I asked him, "Where did you spend the night?"

He said, "Ed's, someone from work."

He didn't come home again that night, it was Christmas Eve.

The marriage counselor called, and said Greg was coming to have a session with him even though it was Christmas Eve. The marriage counselor asked if I was coming to the session with him.

I said, "No, I didn't know about the appointment and didn't think he wanted me there."

The counselor said he thought I should come also. I drove to the counselor's office and left Brit and Case with my mother.

When Greg arrived he said, "What are you doing here?"

He didn't want to meet with me and the counselor. The counselor said he would take Greg in first to talk.

Before they went into the office I said, "What's going on? Are you involved with someone else? Are you sleeping with someone else?"

He didn't answer me. I knew by the look on his face the answer was yes. I ran out of the office crying. I drove home to pick up my mother, and my four children, as we were going to drive to spend Christmas with my family, instead of them coming to Walnut Creek. Greg came to the house to pick up some things, but when he realized we were still there he drove away. On our way to my family we went to visit Greg's parents so they could see the kids for Christmas. I told his parents about our problems, not going into details.

His mother said, "Do you want his dad to talk to him?"

I said, "No."

I was not sure this would help and thought it would only anger him and make things worse. I thought his dad would have a talk with him anyway no matter what I said. It was not a good Christmas. I spent all of my time crying. I hadn't done any shopping, I just gave money as gifts to my children. My son FJ gave me some flowers at the dinner table. He left to pick them up Christmas morning since he hadn't bought any gifts. They looked like they had been run over by a truck, but his heart was there. I laughed until I cried. He was glad they made me laugh again. I left Case with mother and dad, as I had to take my older son and daughter back to Southern California, and Brit came with me. I saw our friends and partners in the home we had moved from. The wife was very supportive, but I know she was worried about how our marriage problems might affect their buying our house.

I called Greg and asked if he wanted to come back and work on our relationship.

His response was, "I need to find myself. We don't have anything in common. You don't like sports and you don't like rock and roll."

When we married I thought he was a mature and responsible person until he gave me those reasons for leaving our children and our marriage. I knew when we married he hadn't had much experience with other women, and one day he might want to sow his wild oats. He was going to turn thirty the end of December, and this seemed to be a time of change for him. I was not going to start divorce proceedings for at least six months.

I said, "I think we need time to reflect."

I asked him if he prayed about his decision, and his reply was "Yes."

I guess he received his guidance and was going ahead with his plans, and served me with divorce papers immediately. He had a friend who was going to law school in San Diego. I remember him making a call to him one evening while we were still together, which I thought was unusual. He never called him just to talk. I later realized that he needed to know the name of an attorney in our area that he could call for the divorce.

I have prayed most of my life for strength and guidance and help in my decisions. I remember when I was four years old I wrote a letter to my grandmother and Jesus in heaven. My dad or my mother must have told me she had gone to heaven to be with Jesus, and my dad was leaving to go to Ohio for the funeral. Mother was in bed after just delivering my baby sister, and I was in my little chair writing a letter to her. My grandmother was the person who took me to church so it made sense to me to write her a letter in heaven. I think she was the one who instilled my belief in prayer and going to church. Growing up we always said grace before meals and at night said our prayers before going to sleep. After she passed away neither of my parents took us to church. It was after my parents' divorce that my younger sisters and I went to church, from the time I was eight. It must have been something that I needed as I searched for a normal life. No one in our neighborhood was divorced I was sure. I don't remember anyone in elementary school being in the same situation.

Divorce Papers

After being served with divorce papers and receiving no regular support from Greg, I knew that I needed an attorney. I got the name of an attorney other friends had used for their divorce. Since she was a female attorney, I thought she would be more supportive. I had to give her $1,000 as a retainer. It was the only money left in the savings account. Unfortunately, it wasn't a good fit, she was not able to give me the time I thought was needed. I asked others in the church singles group for a referral and found another attorney. I knew Greg wasn't going to help me financially. He wanted me to get a job so he wouldn't be required to pay me support. He finally gave me fifty dollars a week when it was convenient for him, for food, diapers, gas, and babysitters while I looked for work. He stopped paying the house payment and it was six months behind at one time. He refused to pay the property taxes and had even said he was going to have the utilities turned off. I couldn't believe he would be so mean and evil-spirited. He thought I was dragging my heels by not finding employment so he would have less financial responsibility. Unemployment was at its highest rate at the time (10%), and there was a hiring freeze on in the government so I couldn't go back to work there. Along with that I was having a difficult time getting more than a few hours of sleep at night, since I was still getting up with both of my children. Greg only wanted to pick the kids up every other weekend, so I was not going to have much help with their physical care either.

I told him, "You can desert me, but you are not going to desert them and go raise someone else's children. I will follow you wherever you go. You will help me raise them." A friend of mine told me when he was going through his divorce, the judge told him he didn't need to pay so much child support. He told the judge he wanted to make sure his children didn't suffer due to their divorce—an example of someone who made the honorable choice.

I told him I wanted to have joint custody. We could

each have them half the time. I even thought we could live in the same neighborhood. That way they could go to the same babysitter and the same school and not have as much disruption. I told him one option was the children could stay in the same house and we could each move out every other week or on a two-week basis. I bought books on this plan and how it worked for others and gave him the books to consider. Since he was living on the other side of the bay now and didn't plan on living in the Walnut Creek area, it wasn't something he wanted to consider. We could still work with a schedule for each of us to have them for two weeks and then two weeks off until they started to school.

I thought back and tried to analyze what had happened to our marriage, and I recalled one instance when I was pregnant and Greg was on a trip out of town. I was waiting for his return. He was late, and I had fallen asleep on the couch. I had a dream that he died, and I woke up crying. That dream made me think I was all alone again and would be raising our children on my own. I think somehow my subconscious was telling me something was wrong, but I was not looking at the signs.

He was the one that kept pursuing me and wanted to get married. After two and a half years I accepted his proposal.

When I met Greg, I had a love interest in Africa. We met before my friend took an assignment in Kenya, Africa for two years. He sent me a ticket to come and visit him, and it was a great trip. We camped all over the area, but couldn't go into Uganda and Tanzania at the time due to the restrictions on travel. It was after that I decided to apply to the State Department and join him and other friends who were there. I received a call from the State Department for a position in Kenya. I told my older son and daughter about the job offer, but they would have to go away to English boarding schools. My daughter thought that sounded exciting, but my son was adamant that he didn't want to go to boarding school. I thought about taking him and if he was not happy I would send him back to his father to live. In the end, I decided I didn't want to split the family up to take the job. After reading some of the experiences of the boys and the trauma they went through at some boarding schools, I am glad that I didn't follow through with the job offer.

Because my friend's jobs were related to weather modification there was a great deal of down time. He and his friend used this time thinking of ways to increase their wealth when they returned to the US. While in Africa, my friend helped me shop for souvenirs to take back to friends and family. These were wooden animal miniatures, such as elephants, rhinoceros, and various other animals. His thinking was that tanzanite was going to become more valuable as it became scarcer. He thought I could take some stones back to the US hidden in my animals. He thought I had an honest face and customs wouldn't suspect me of not declaring these items. He didn't know me well enough to know that all the officials had to do was look at me, and I would surrender and say, "I give up." So that was not going to work. I started having nightmares about going to jewelry stores to sell these stones. Then the criminal element in our town, knowing that I had valuable stones in my home, would be coming to see me with guns. After my dreams I told him I couldn't take part in his plan, and the nightmares stopped.

Another time he asked me if I would take money out of the country for some friends of his from India. Kenya was forcing all non-natives to leave their property and assets when they left the country. I thought about it and decided even though I was sympathetic to their plight I could not participate in that request. I could see down the road there could be a dispute about how much money they gave me and wondered how I would resolve that situation. Plus, there was the fact that I did not want to go to jail for bringing their money into the US. I had two children to consider. Many times, women get into these situations thinking they are helping someone out even though it is illegal and end up ruining their life.

Greg saw a letter from him in my purse, and asked me what was going on. By then I was sure that my love interest relationship from Africa was over. He was going back to Kansas to help his dad with the wheat farm. For many years I had dreams that I returned to Africa to see him, but I never did. Once, when I had a layover in Kansas I called him to meet me for coffee, but when I found out he had been in a relationship for some time, I decided not to pursue that any further.

One of the men we worked with accused Greg of marrying me because I had a house. He became defensive, and told me he protested that had nothing to do with our marrying. Was that an incentive for him to marry me since it would increase his net worth? Was he just in the marriage until someone else came along? One therapist told me that marriages are tested more at the birth of a second child and the divorce rate is higher at that time. I guess I wasn't paying attention to signals he was giving me.

~~~~~~~~

New Year's Eve: *December 31, 1981*

I decided I needed to do something for New Year's Eve to lift my spirits. Mother encouraged me to go out, as she would be able to watch the children. I read in the newspaper about a home party for singles and decided to attend. I wanted to meet other people in the area and this was a good way to start. It took a great deal of talking to myself to get my courage up to go alone, but after I was there I felt comfortable, as they were a nice group of people. I overheard a conversation about a singles group that met at a church, and I asked for more information and learned they met every Sunday evening. When I asked for the directions, they said just follow all the cars off of the freeway exit, as they are all going to the church on Sunday night.

That Sunday after New Year's I decided to attend the singles meeting at the Presbyterian Church. I saw on the agenda one of the featured speakers was our marriage counselor. I wanted to hear him speak. I thought I would gain some insight into what he had said to Greg, and why Greg decided to leave our marriage. Since I was new to the group it was recommended that I attend the meeting for new people. When I first went in and sat down I was fine. We all sat in a big circle, each telling their particular situation of concern. It all seemed so hopeless. I left feeling very low, and I'm sure the leaders in the group weren't sure I would ever come back again. Many years later I was at a Toastmaster's meeting and learned something about our marriage counselor.

He was asked if he believed in monogamy and his answer was, "Women want men to be monogamous, but men aren't able to be."

I couldn't believe this was the counselor we went to for help in our relationship. Were we doomed from the beginning because we picked a counselor that didn't believe in commitment. I guess that's what happens when you pick a marriage counselor out of the yellow pages, but I didn't know anyone in the area to ask for a referral.

It took a couple of weeks to work up my courage to go back to the singles meeting for a second time. I decided to attend again when a friend from the newcomer's group called me and said she was going. She said she wanted to "fall in love again." She had been to these meetings before and always met someone and "fell in love." Her husband left her for another woman from his office so we experienced similar circumstances in our marriages. We went to the Sunday night program and then afterwards to one of the local restaurants that had music where most of the group usually frequented. She eventually met someone and fell in love.

~~~~~~~~~

Superbowl Sunday

Superbowl Sunday Greg was to pick up our children. I dropped mother off at her job. She was a caregiver for people in the retirement community. I waited at home for him and he didn't show up. I called Sister Anne at the Bay Area Crisis Nursery. She gave a talk at our church and was very compassionate. She said if I needed help I could bring the children and leave them with her for however long I needed and I would be able to pick them up whenever I wanted. I was very depressed at that point. Sundays were always the hardest time to be alone. I waited over two hours for Greg and when he didn't show up or call I took them to the Crisis Nursery and left them with Sister Anne. I felt very comfortable at the Nursery, it was very calming and very peaceful. Sister Anne had a way of soothing me when she talked, and was nonjudgmental. All I wanted was to go for a walk, and to have a few minutes to myself. Brit was having a difficult time with the turmoil in our life, and I was still recovering from the birth of Case. After I went for a long walk around the lake at the park I stopped at the golf course to have a glass of wine, forgetting it was Superbowl Sunday. I didn't want to be reminded that I didn't like football. I had spent so many times with Greg's family watching football, baseball, golf, or whatever other sports event was on at the time. There didn't seem much time talking within the family.

While working full-time and attending classes to finish my bachelor's degree, in addition on weekends I had to study, do homework, laundry, housecleaning, and yard work. Before we were married when Greg was at my house for the weekend and I was studying he would have the football game on with the sound off. I never complained or said anything about him watching football. If not studying I used that time to read, sew, or work on my ceramics.

At the golf course restaurant, I had a glass of wine while looking out the window observing the park below. There was a couple close by having brunch, they seemed so enamored of each other, and I envied them. I remembered seeing them at the single's meeting previously. It was not easy to keep myself from crying, but every time I went out of the house there were so many reminders of the loss in my life. I seemed to be crying all the time. Some people from another table sent me a glass of wine, and I thanked them for it. Then they invited me to join them. I wasn't dressed for meeting people, I had on my baggy jogging suit and tennis shoes. When I came home Greg left a note for me, he had let himself in the house since he still had his key, and waited for me to return. He called the next day and wanted to know where Brit and Case were. I told him they were being taken care of by Sister Anne. When I left our children at the Crisis Nursery one of my neighbors, who was a volunteer helper, saw me come in and leave my children. I think she was embarrassed for me. She called me and came over later that night to talk. We had been to her house for dinner in a gourmet dinner group we belonged to, so she knew Greg. I told Sister Anne I would be picking them up later that day, as I was feeling more in control of myself now. I just needed a little help once in a while and couldn't get it from their father. That was one of the lowest points in my life during the divorce and separation. I never again left them with Sister Anne at the Crisis Nursery, or anyone else. I always promised that I would return the help they had given me. When I was responsible for the Combined Federal Campaign at work I called Sister Anne, and she

BARBARA SHAW

gave a presentation on how her group helps families. They did not receive government funding so I hoped this would encourage donations to her organization.

~~~~~~~~~~~~~~~~

Case's Baptism

It was my birthday and I decided it was time to have Case baptized. I told their dad about the plans but he chose not to attend. I dreaded standing up at the altar by myself with Case, but several of the women from church stood up beside me to give me moral support. Mother was able to attend and then I took her to work, so then it was just Brit, Case, and I. Sundays were difficult to deal with. Many times, I wanted someone to talk to. Brit was still having a difficult time since she did not understand why her dad left. She had frequent crying spells. I know she didn't understand why things changed so much. When we went out before the separation she was always smiling, people always commented on her smiling. Now when we went out she thought people did not like her, her self-image had been affected by all this. I tried to keep them busy by going to the park, to McDonald's for a burger, or to feed the horses up the road by Mt. Diablo. I tried anything to keep our minds off of our situation. I joined some other mothers in the area who would get together and talk while our children played. I learned a good lesson from one of the mothers. She said she had to get herself and her children out of the house by 10 a.m. before the "ten o'clock crazies" set in. So that was my goal and I stayed with it. I needed to get out of the house so I didn't dwell on the many problems and decisions I needed to make. Dwelling on all of the "what ifs" would sometimes be overwhelming. Fresh air and sunshine always helped me and my children.

Since the separation I had not been able to eat and lost fifty pounds after my son was born. Food just seemed to stick in my throat and wouldn't go down. I wasn't able to sleep through the night yet, as Case was still waking up. My mother would get up with him and change him and give him a bottle and then I would do the same, but I was only getting a couple of hours of sleep at a time.

I think the lack of sleep and the weight loss affected my thinking. I was driving to see my family and I passed over a bridge and had thoughts of ending it all then and there with my children. I knew this insanity would pass if I could just make it through one more day. I would feel differently if I could just get enough rest and eat properly. I couldn't do something stupid like that to my children and my family. When I was about eleven years old, the man next door committed suicide. The newspaper said he was found in his car in the front of their house and had put a hose from the exhaust to the window. He left behind four children and they had to carry that burden for the rest of their lives. I remember how sad they were and how hard it was for them. I didn't want to leave my children with that to deal with the rest of their lives. Many years later my sister made a comment that they didn't think I was going to make it. I just kept praying and saying to myself I just needed to get through this day. Tomorrow would be better.

I had been responsible for my two younger sisters

from the time I was seven years old due to divorce of my parents. My sisters depended on me to carry on and make things better during our childhood. I can only guess that they didn't know how to help me in my time of need. I think some people where I attended church probably felt the same way. The women would call me and volunteer to take my children while I went out and ran errands or went for a walk. What I wanted most was just their friendship, someone to talk to and to be part of a group for me and my children.

One person that was a great help to me was Lin. She said to me, "It's not only the women in church who are behind you, but the men are also there for you for what you are going through."

I was very touched by that comment. When her husband died there seemed to be a great deal of support for her and her children. I think it was easier for them to help a widow than a divorcee. So, I ended up spending a great deal of time driving back to family and friends, and trying to decide where to live when we sold the house. My cup was empty and the only way I could get the love and support I needed was with people who knew me when I was happy and whole, not broken and depressed. I had not made friends yet in Walnut Creek so it was very lonely for me, but I knew I was so lucky to have my mother with me. I never felt as good after the birth of any of my other children as I did this time, and it was because she was with me. It helped me gain my strength physically and mentally for all the emotional turmoil I would be experiencing. I owed a lot to her for being with me and will always be grateful to her for helping me through the most difficult time in my life. She hadn't always been there for me growing up, but this made up for all those times. I know I would have probably ended it all if it hadn't been for her being there with me. She saved me and my children—otherwise I might have made another decision.

~~~~~~~~~~

The Roommates

I decided to run an ad to see if I could find someone to help me with childcare so I could look for work. I could only offer a sitter room and board in exchange for childcare. I interviewed several people, and I chose Sy. She was a light-skinned African-American woman who worked in the day, didn't party or drink and the only other place she went was to church. The arrangement was that she would sit for me on her days off and also in the evening. This worked out for me since I had taken a job selling timeshares for condos in Hawaii and most of the appointments were in the evenings when both spouses were at home. It was winter time, but when I was working or had an appointment I had to wear my Hawaiian shirt to keep with the theme. I am sure my neighbors were wondering what kind of job I had that I would dress this way. My job entailed meeting at a nice restaurant, having dinner with a group of three to four couples, and then making an appointment to sell them a timeshare for Hawaii.

Staying at home without any adult conversation was not easy. I was still depressed about the divorce and trying to make decisions for our lives. My goal was to get through a day without breaking down and sobbing. Going to work and interacting with other adults meant I had to keep myself together and not lose it out in public. Since it was a commission only job it was not long before I decided that this job was not going to work out for me. I needed gas money and it would be sometime before I was going to have a sale. I asked Greg to exchange cars with me since the Volkswagen would have better gas mileage than the big Chevy Caprice I was driving. He wasn't interested in making the exchange with me, but later changed his mind and I felt he must be having problems with the car and wanted to dump it on me. We installed air conditioning after buying the car and had problems with it overheating since then. Soon after that he bought another car.

~~~~~~~~~~~~~~~~~

Tax Returns

Greg wanted us to file together, as it would mean a better tax break for us. When he brought the returns to me I signed them both thinking he would not be able to cash the refund checks without my signature. I was wrong. He cashed the check, forged my name, and deposited the refund to his account. This could have caused him some problems at work since. There was nothing I could do; the money was already in his account. I wanted to write a letter to the IRS telling them about his forging my name to the checks, but was talked out of it by my attorney. My attorney thought he could lose his job, then I would have no support, but in the end the support he gave was not dependable. He paid the child support when it was convenient for him, and for the first six months after he left that was only fifty dollars per week for food, diapers, formula, and gas in order to find a job.

CHAPTER TWO

Prayer, Music and Sailing

One of the ways I was able to hold on for tomorrow was my ability to pray and connect with God. I had to keep believing that I would be able to get over this horrible experience. I prayed constantly. When I drove across country with my two older children, who were six and seven years old, people asked me how did I make it by myself. I told them the good Lord and I were always in communication. I drove through tornados in Louisiana. I had a blowout in Houston and had to walk to the gas station with both my children for help changing my tire. My tire was almost stolen since I left it beside my car while we walked to the gas station. As we drove up to the car someone was getting ready to grab my tire, but sped away when we showed up in the tow truck. The people in Houston were so helpful I thought of staying there, but my family was in California. My car wouldn't start in Albuquerque and I had to wait for the gas station to open up to get a jump for my battery. From then on, I only stopped at gas stations in case I had the same thing happen again. We ate peanut butter sandwiches or whatever we found available at the gas station. I had to drive through sand storms in Arizona and my car was rocking back and forth due to the weight of the U-Haul luggage rack I had on my hood. I was sent out of my way by AAA in case of snow, and since my snow tire was the one that I had a blowout on, I now only had one snow tire. I drove for seventeen hours from Albuquerque until I arrived at my sisters' and was exhausted. Prayer got me through this trip, which my daughter remembers as the trip from hell.

When I was very, very depressed I prayed constantly asking for strength and courage to get through the court cases with the divorce and custody. My greatest time of need came when I was walking during my lunch hour, and I prayed please dear Lord take this burden from me or take me. I can't bear this pain anymore. I can say in all my years of praying I have never had such an immediate relief. I felt the pain lift from me. Psychologists and psychiatrists might be able to explain why this happened. My pain was so bad that my brain was ready to accept the relief I felt immediately. I am not sure I will ever experience that again. Maybe we only get one of those experiences when we are really, really low.

Another time, I was walking in San Francisco and heard church bells and tried to find out where they were coming from. It took me several days of walking to find the church, as I had been going in circles. The church had a noon service every day for workers in the city, and this was a great source of spiritual nourishment to me. I later joined this church when I moved to the city.

Greg told me he thought I was a better Christian than he was. I don't know why he said that since he was raised a Catholic. I thought of one instance when he saw my values being tested when we were traveling before we were married, and I found a wallet at the airline counter. After looking in the wallet and seeing four $100 bills, an airline ticket, and no identification, I turned it in to the airline and their comment was, "Boy are we going to have a party."

I told them, "If anyone was going to have a party it was me."

I turned the wallet over to the airline employee, but wondered if the correct person received their wallet with the cash included. Was this when he based his opinion of me as a Christian?

I also used meditation which was a great help to get my brain working with positive messages. A friend of mine who was Buddhist said that he sang verses from the Bible in the morning to ensure he started his day positively, which I adopted.

I am not a perfect person, just ask my children, or my family. They know all of my flaws. None of us are perfect, we all have our dark side. All I can do is try to treat others as I would want to be treated.

The other way I was able to get my life back was to take guitar lessons. My older daughter had a guitar when she was in junior high. She took lessons, but gave up after a short while. When we moved to Walnut Creek I decided to take lessons, since it was something I had thought of doing for some time. I wanted to play classical guitar and found someone close by to give me lessons. When I went for my second lesson, I was kept waiting while she was meeting with a couple for their wedding. I finally had to leave, as I could see this was going to take too much time, and in addition to paying for the lessons I was also paying for a babysitter. After that I met someone in the singles group who gave guitar lessons and lived close by. She always said it was therapeutic to play guitar, because you can't sing and cry at the same time. I kept up my lessons with her and joined a guitar class at the adult education group in Pleasant Hill, that met once a week. It was very uplifting to sing and play with a group. At the end of the semester the class went to the local pizza parlor, we played guitar, sang, and ate pizza. I know there were times I was crying while I was playing, but kept going.

I gave one of my guitars to Brit when she went to college, along with songs and the music, and a guitar tuner. I told her this would be a good way to meet other people and to keep from getting lonely until she made friends. She said that it was hard to keep the guitar in-tune because of the humidity. I told her to play with music on CDs that she liked and not to worry about keeping it in-tune all the time. It doesn't always have to be perfectly in-tune.

I was very lucky to find a sailing club that was just starting up in Walnut Creek when my son was six months old. I went to the first meeting and joined immediately. The dues were fifty dollars per month and this covered a guaranteed sail once a month and more if there were dropouts. The schedule was made and the soonest I would be scheduled for a sail was the next month. Not wanting to wait to sail, and since my weekend coming up was Greg's weekend with the children, I decided to drive to Southern California and stay with my older son in his camper and sail with the Marina del Rey group. I was very lucky that day that I met a lady in the group who must have been a social worker, and I started talking to her like I would my mother. I was so glad then that I hadn't done something foolish that might have me end up in jail and not enjoying the beautiful day sailing, with the sunshine and breeze in my face. It was the best therapy money could buy.

I have always been a walker. As a child we didn't have money for a bus, so we walked wherever we wanted to go. I always knew that exercise was important for my mental health, and tried to get out for walks in the fresh air every day. I knew when I came back home after walking it helped clear my mind. If I was having any problems I knew that I just had to keep walking to get myself back into a better frame of mind. I would walk at lunch time when I was working and, in the evening, when I was home after work.

Many times, I said, "If things get worse I am going to have to walk to Canada."

That was always my plan B, just keep walking until my mind was clear of negativity.

CHAPTER THREE

First Roommate

At the time I interviewed for childcare I interviewed a young man who wanted the position. When I told him I hired someone, he asked since he didn't get the job if he could rent a room from me. I thought this would be a way to help my financial needs. I had never done this before, only living with family and my children. As it turned out I was one of the first homeowners in the Bay Area who rented rooms. He was the first of my many roommates over the eighteen years I lived there.

He seemed to be okay and after I checked out his references I let him move in one of the extra bedrooms by mother. I came home one day and there were hard boiled eggs all over the kitchen walls, ceiling, counters, and floor. I went to several of my neighbors and asked had they seen anyone at my house. It was a mystery to me because I knew everyone was usually at work. I finally figured out what happened. He had come home for lunch and put eggs on to cook. He forgot he left them on the stove and when the pan ran out of water, the eggs exploded. It would be much later in the evening before he would be home, but I was not going to clean up his mess. One of his jobs was to clean houses, in addition to his job as a paramedic. He was at home the weekend I went to Southern California to be with my older daughter on her birthday. Greg was to pick up the kids for the weekend, so my mother would not have to watch them. When I came back on Sunday night he told me my mother had chest pains and they called an ambulance and she was taken to the hospital. I knew she had been drinking while I was gone, as she was having a problem dealing with the stress of the divorce. I was in my room when mother came in and laid down on the bed beside me to talk about what happened with her heart attack episode. I didn't want to listen to her excuses. I was sure that her drinking was responsible for her heart incident. I was angry at her for drinking while I was gone. After this episode my mother decided to move back closer to my sisters. I was sorry to see her go, but helped her pack her things and drove her back to a friend she was going to be staying with until she was able to find something more permanent.

~~~~~~~~~~~~~~~

Kelly, Our Irish Setter

When we moved to the Bay Area we brought Kelly, our Irish Setter, with us. We inherited him from a former neighbor. The neighbor was a single mother and was moving from Southern California to Placerville. She planned to drive a moving truck with her furniture, other belongings and her two small children to their new home and was going to put Kelly in the dog pound. He was such a big dog that I didn't think he would be adopted and it was a mutual agreement to keep him. When Greg was away on business I always felt secure with Kelly around. He was an extremely large Irish Setter, and he would not let anyone into the house or yard. After Greg left it was difficult for me to take Kelly for walks and get his exercise with a baby and a toddler, and the yard was too small for such a big dog. I called our former neighbor, and she had reunited with her husband and expressed an interest in taking him back. Since she had more help and support than I did at this time I thought it would be a better home for Kelly to be with them. She and her husband came while I was out and took Kelly back with them that weekend.

~~~~~~~~~~~

Roommate Leaves

After that I had to have the house sprayed because of fleas from Kelly, and had to leave with the kids for the weekend. My roommate decided to move out at this time, as he was concerned about the chemicals. If I had known this was all I had to do to get him to leave I would have had the house sprayed sooner. My childcare worker was staying and said she would take care of things while I was away and I knew I could depend on her. When I came home I noticed some things were missing; the television cable box, a video game, the cooler and the sleeping bags. Greg would come into the house and take whatever he wanted and then when I went looking for something I would call him and find out he had taken the item. I later found out that Greg had taken the sleeping bags and the cooler. I told him I needed the cooler for the children for when I took them to the park. I had to take juice, bottles and snacks for them whenever we went out of the house. We bought those sleeping bags for camping, since they zipped together I couldn't believe he would think another woman would want to use my sleeping bag. It would be like wearing another woman's underwear and imagining that we had been intimate in them.

When I asked about the missing items, Sy called the former roommate and told him she had taken responsibility for the house while I was away, and this reflected on her integrity and honesty. He brought back some of the things he had taken, except for the video game. The video game was in a box in the garage and in order to hide his theft he stuffed the box with newspapers to appear heavy. I didn't realize for some time later that it was missing, by then it was too late to do anything. It was a small price to pay for having him leave. When he left he put a bullet on the desk in his room. I guess this was intended to be a message for me. I knew he was suspected of stealing from some of the houses he cleaned, but I don't think they were able to prove anything at the time. I decided not to make a police report. The items he had taken were minor and I did not want to have any more contact with him. He talked about some of the things he did to patients as a paramedic and could have been fired for, but I guess no one made a formal complaint against him. He could be an evil person when he wanted to. His demeanor was very confusing. He seemed likeable, and was trying to get his life together by working two jobs. I believe the house cleaning jobs were just a way to get into homes easy and take what he thought he could get away with.

~~~~~~

Temporary Employment

In order to work I took temporary jobs through various employment agencies, but had to find someone to take care of our children in the day time. I called several employment agencies for a sitter since I didn't know anyone in the area. I counted on these sitters to be screened, and references checked. This worked for a while, but it was really too expensive. Once when I came home from work my daughter came rushing up to me and was so happy, she said, "Look Mommy I found your book, it was under the chair." I usually left my journal under the chair out of sight and where I could get to it easily for when I felt like writing. A friend from church had given me the journal as a gift, and I started writing in it some of the things that were going on, as well as what my thoughts and feelings. One look at the sitter's face and I knew she had read my personal journal. I guess that is one of the reasons I didn't want to keep a journal of private feelings and have someone read them without my permission.

One of my neighbors babysat for me a few times, but I couldn't count on her for full-time. She ended up making more money than I did, but that is one of the problems working mothers have. I couldn't take them to a regular childcare facility because I only worked on an intermittent basis. I put my application in for several government vacancies since most of the private industry jobs in Walnut Creek were going to women who could work for less. At the time most of the government agencies were having a hiring freeze, so it was taking longer to find a position. I went on several interviews and received the same polite replies, sorry. I interviewed for a position in Walnut Creek for an attorney, and something about the name was familiar. When I asked for one of the business cards of the office, I realized this was the office of Greg's attorney. The attorney conducting the interview was impressed with my resume and said he wanted to hire me. He said he would talk to the other attorney, but I knew there was no chance they were going to hire me. Greg's attorney was probably going to have to rip me up in court and this would put them in an awkward position.

Jen, Roommate

I needed someone who was available for more hours of babysitting in the evening while I was selling timeshares, and I decided to place another ad for a sitter in exchange for a room. I had no income yet, since the timeshares were a commission only position. I selected a young girl just out of high school. She was working as a receptionist part-time and needed additional work. After she moved in I went to church for a new members class. While sitting in my car I could see all the couples in the room. I started feeling unsure if I could hold it together and not start crying. I sat in the parking lot trying to decide what to do. I was working on getting my courage up to go in and join the group, but went home instead. I heard voices in the kitchen, but went upstairs to my room, not wanting to talk to anyone. When I came upstairs I heard Brit crying, but could tell she would be going to sleep soon, and so I went into my room. I was in the bathroom and I heard shouting. I went to the hall and I heard Jen the sitter in my daughter's room, calling her names. I went into the room, she turned around and was surprised to see me. I didn't say anything. I went past her, picked Brit up, took her into my bedroom, comforted her and kept her there for the night. The next day when I was in the kitchen, I had Case in my arms and was fixing a bottle for him. I told her I don't think this position was going to work out. I would give her two weeks to find another place to live. She wanted to argue with me how it was not her fault. She went on and on and got very ugly towards me. I left the kitchen and went into the family room with Case and she followed me. I told her that the two weeks was no longer an option, and she needed to be out immediately. I think she would have hit me if I hadn't been holding Case. She couldn't move back with her family, because they had a rule that when you were eighteen and graduated from high school you had to move out, that was the rule, and there were no exceptions. It wasn't an easy move, things were tense until she moved out. She blamed me for her problems, claiming it was all my fault. When she moved she took a bottle of scotch and a Sara Lee cheesecake. It's always been amazing to me what some people will take when they move out. This was her way of getting even with me, I guess.

Sy Takes Over Again

I had taken another temporary job close to home and by then Sy was no longer working and needed full-time work. Since she was home during the day she could take care of my children, and I could pay her in addition to her room. I was at work when I received a call from someone in my church. She told me my neighbor was going to call child welfare because my babysitter was not watching my children. Brit had been out in the cul-de-sac playing in the street and fallen asleep in the driveway. I raced home from work to see what was going on. I told Sy that from now on Brit was not to go out front and play even though we lived on a cul-de-sac with very little traffic. I fixed up the backyard with a sand box, her slide and a swing. Several times I came home from work and Sy had taken the children with her when she went to church. I always worried about someone kidnapping them even when they were with her. Case was very loving and would go to most people. I don't know if he was loved so much because he was born lovable or he became lovable because he was loved so much by all he met. Brit lost her happy face after the divorce. She didn't smile, she thought people didn't like her, her self-esteem was greatly damaged. She loved her dad and wanted us all to be a family again. She told me her dad wanted to come back, and I told her no, her dad was never coming back. I told Greg he needed to talk to her so she wouldn't go on with false hopes about us being a family again.

My neighbors and Greg were curious as to how my sitter was able to drive a new model Cadillac. She told me before she moved in that the Cadillac was a present to herself when she retired. She was a good person, but not a worker, her heart was really not in the job. The minute I came home in the evening she was out the door. If I did anything in the evening I had to take the kids with me. One problem was their meals. It usually took them longer to finish their food. I told her she could leave their meal on the table for a short time and they would come back and finish it later. When I came home from work the food from breakfast and lunch were still on the table. I guess she took this literally. Once I made plans to go to a meeting for a weekend singles trip and thought she would be home, but when I got home she dashed out the door. I finally told her that I would find someone else for child-care and gave her two weeks notice. She could continue to live at my house, but I would have to charge her rent. After that she decided to find another arrangement.

Weekend at Mendocino

There was a singles group that was going to Mendocino for the weekend and the meeting before the trip was to discuss carpooling, sleeping, and food assignments. I had to find someone to watch the kids. Greg said he could not do it, as he had plans. I called Lin from church and asked if she could manage them for the weekend in addition to her five children. She always felt close to them and helped me when she could. She said she and her husband would adopt them if we didn't think we could raise them. I told her that they should be with me and their dad, we weren't thinking about giving them up. At the time, her husband was receiving dialysis after a kidney transplant and was given tainted blood from a donor. She said he needed another kidney and I volunteered to donate a kidney to him. Since the first one didn't take the doctors said he needed one from a family member. He didn't last much longer. It was a sad time for them and for everyone who knew him.

CHAPTER FOUR

Ro: *August 1982*

I was still looking for work, but had not found anything permanent. I had gone out for the evening and left word with the babysitter that I would be up the street at a gathering with the singles group. I sat at the bar for a while talking to some of the group and the bar's phone rang. I was concerned that the babysitter would be needing help and calling. I asked if the caller was asking for me, and the bartender said, no they were not. I stayed a couple of hours and then went home with a friend following me for a cup of coffee. When we got to the house, there was a message from my youngest sister in Oklahoma. I called her back immediately and she told me there had been an accident. Ro, her son, only three years old, had been hit by a car and didn't survive. They were bringing his body back from Oklahoma for the funeral. It was a sad day for all of us. Such a lovely, happy child, taken away so suddenly. I said goodbye to my friend, he didn't know what to say or how to react. I am sure he had never walked into a situation like that. I left the next day to be there when they arrived. My other sister was in Shasta Lake on vacation and was expected back Sunday evening. They did not know the awful news. She and her husband were going to be devastated. They were so close to Ro. They were his substitute parents whenever Prip needed a break or someone to watch him. When Prip's husband took the job in Oklahoma, he left the job of selling the house to her. She had to work full-time, take care of the house and the children. I went to visit her several times since I wasn't working and Brit and Ro really enjoyed one another. At times they were happy and laughing and then they would be at one another fighting for the same toy. I had asked Nk, Prip's older daughter to take them out for a walk and after just a few minutes she returned, she was finished. Prip remembered the way I had to take care of her and Lynn when we were growing up, and she did not want her daughter to have that great a responsibility. Later I found out Ro had been hit by a car while my sister was ironing, and he was outside riding his hot wheels out of the driveway into the street. Their house didn't have sidewalks and they lived on a busy street. She heard the sound of screeching tires and went out to find him on the street, hit by a car driven by a twenty-year-old female. She called for an ambulance, and they took him by helicopter to the hospital, but he didn't survive. It had taken several days to bring his body to the funeral, and by then his body had started to deteriorate. They decided to have an open casket and at the viewing he looked like an old man. He started to turn gray because of the time elapsed since his death. The Pastor that spoke knew my sister Lynn and her husband, as he had spoken at another funeral. His message was a great source of comfort to all. Ro was buried in a plot next to Lynn's father-in-law. After the funeral I left to take my mother and father back to their place. I called Prip to say goodbye, but was not able to talk because I was crying. She said, "I know you're there because I can hear you crying." I knew if I said goodbye to her at the funeral I would not be able to stop crying. I went home knowing that I needed to start looking for a job again, if just to get me out of the house for my peace of mind.

***

Vi

My good friend Vi called me after Case was born and she noticed something wrong in my voice. We had worked together previously. My older children and I stayed with her a few months while our house was being built. She was my maid of honor when Greg and I got married, and we stayed in touch as we both moved to different locations. After you know someone for over thirty-plus years, I guess when there are problems it comes across on the phone.

She asked my mother, "Was I okay, or was I just recuperating from delivering Case just two years after Brit's birth?"

Vi didn't know about the separation. I didn't want to share too much and then be sorry later and look foolish. She knew I was looking for work and she had been looking out for jobs available in my area. She sent me vacancy announcements if she thought I qualified and they were in my commuting area. I applied for a position in the city from an announcement she sent me and I was waiting to hear from them for an interview. They hadn't been able to reach me for some reason and called an office in Los Angeles where I had previously been employed. Luckily, they talked to a lady who knew me and gave them my telephone number. She called me to see how things were going and if I was okay. She had sent me a baby blanket, sweater and cap for Case she knitted. She knew when I didn't send back a thank you note something was wrong. She worked with Greg in Southern California, and was really disappointed in his behavior for leaving me and our children.

I received a call for an interview from the branch head and went into the city for an interview. It was a great job for me to start back in, as my boss and the other employees always kept me laughing. It was like a family. I stayed in this position longer than I intended because of the atmosphere. My boss always complimented me on my skills and how fast I was getting jobs done. He didn't want the other offices to know how skilled I was or they would be calling on me to do their work, as their employees weren't as efficient. I told him many times he should give me a high-quality award, but that wasn't his style. Later, at other offices where I worked and received awards I reminded him I deserved one when I was working in his office and he agreed. I had taken this job because it was right on the BART path and I would have an easy commute. Once I was in the office I found out about a van pool which was going to save me money and time, so I joined them.

Bett Moves In: *June 1982*

Bett, my oldest daughter, had graduated from high school, and I traveled several times to bring her to Walnut Creek, but she wanted to stay where her friends were. She and her brother FJ moved in together in an apartment with some of her friends. Her dad was sending her the twenty-five dollars per week child support so she could stay until she graduated. After she graduated she wanted to stay and try to make it on her own. She didn't want to make the move with us when we moved to Northern California. I didn't want her to be miserable and unhappy, and decided she could stay with her older brother and friends. I attended five high schools due to family moves and adjusting was difficult, and didn't want her to go through the same thing. I moved out of my mother's apartment due to her drinking problem when I was sixteen and lived on my own. I thought Bett could handle living on her own since she had her brother to help watch over her. I am not sure that was a good decision. I don't think she was mature enough to handle the responsibility with the freedom. She finally decided to move to Walnut Creek when her father's wife stopped sending the child support checks. He trusted his new wife to pay the bills and send the checks on time as he had. When she called her dad, she received the same response, "the check was mailed." She had a part-time job at a Chinese restaurant and did house cleaning to make ends meet, but it was difficult for her when she did not receive the checks as promised.

I was working full-time now and since she needed work, she agreed to babysit during the day and would enroll in the community college for evening classes. I told her I would pay for her tuition and books as long as her grades were average. No Ds or Fs. After coming home a couple of times and finding Case walking around without diapers and the house a mess I knew this was not the job for her. She decided to look for work when the children were with their dad for his two weeks. One weekend she golfed with me, and after golfing we were talking to De about her employment search. He told her he had a vacancy in his department at a bank in the city, and if she was interested he would put in a good word for her. She went in for the interview and was offered the job. This was a beginning of a great opportunity and lasted for several years. She had her own checking account, her own credit card, and her own money. She was meeting people, going out to lunch, and had a great life at last. After she earned enough leave for a vacation she decided to go to Hawaii. She asked several of her friends to go, but they did not have the money, a job, or a credit card. She went by herself and had a great time.

One of my rules when she went out on a date was to call me if she was not going to be coming home. She had gone out before and if she wasn't home I would be up at 2:00 or 3:00 a.m. because I could not sleep due to worrying over where she was and if she was okay. I told her "I am always up, no matter what time it is. I want to know you are okay, and not dead." I would usually be up vacuuming just to get rid of some of my anger, worry and frustration. After a couple of incidents of not calling when she wasn't coming home, I told her that if she continued to do this she could not live with me. I could not stand the anxiety and worry. She knew that she was on thin ice.

~~~~~~~~~~~

Mugging

One morning after I had been on the job for just a month, I was walking in with one of the men from the van pool. I had my head down and was not paying attention to what was going on around me when a man came up and punched me in the face. I screamed in shock and pain. I remembered afterwards he had on purple tennis shoes. I didn't even see his face. One of the men from the van pool took off after the man and some of the people from the van came to my aid and helped me go to the nurse's station. My lip was busted and puffed out. The employee nurse thought I should go have stitches on the inside of my lip, but I said no.

My boss thought I should go home, so he drove me home and helped me pick up my children from the babysitter. I should have stayed at the nurse's station instead, since my home was cold and dark which added to the depressing atmosphere. I left the car keys with one of the men from the van pool to give to Bett since she was part of the van pool also, and able drive my car home. It was very upsetting to her when she got in the van that night to learn what happened to me. My mother and sister Lynn called me later in the day, and I told them what happened. I told them I felt I was lucky that the mugger didn't have an iron pipe or a gun when he hit me in the face. About a month after that when we were going to the van and I noticed a great deal of activity going on. I saw a lady on the ground and one man was chasing another in and out of the traffic. I noticed his shoes were a bright color. I found out later that a woman had been attacked and because she was petite he was able to knock her on the ground and stomp her. She ended up with broken ribs and was in the hospital. I called the police station to see when this man would be going to trial and they told me they didn't have him in the system, that he was probably released due to lack of space. He seemed very cynical, saying "that's the way the system works." Many of the people out on the street had previously been in institutions, but due to the Reagan administration budget cuts, they were released and were not taking their medications to control their aggressive, dangerous behavior.

I went back to the office the next day since I didn't have enough sick leave to take any more time off. I considered work as therapy for me at that time. The heating bills for my home were $300 per month and turning up the heat did not even guarantee that you would be warm. If the sun came out then the house would warm up sometime later in the afternoon, but on a cloudy, rainy or overcast day, the house was cold and damp. Work was the only way I was going to keep my sanity. At work everyone on our floor came by to see how I looked after the attack, and asked what happened.

After that episode I considered buying a gun for protection. I was easily frightened and jumpy for several months. If anyone walked up to me to ask for directions or jogged past me I probably would have shot them. Bett came up behind me and scared me, and if I had that gun

I probably would have shot her by mistake. I did look at guns at a pawn shop and gave it some consideration, but with the divorce going on it was best there wasn't a gun available. I know there many times when my boss walked into the office to see me on the phone with tears in my eyes, but he never asked me about my personal life.

~~~~~~~~

My Goldfish

I bought gold fish for my desk at work to watch for relaxation and once the fish had babies. When I came back to work after the weekend, the babies were gone. The larger fish had probably eaten them.

One of the visitors in our office asked me, "How are the babies doing?"

I said, "They died."

He came over to me and put his arm around me and offered his condolences. When he went in to see my boss, he told him about me losing my "babies." My boss called the other lady in the office to see if she knew anything about my "babies dying." He thought I must be some tough lady to lose her children and still come into work without missing a beat. When they realized I was talking about my goldfish we all had a good laugh.

~~~~~~~~

Jogging

One of the benefits of this office was several of the people in the office were joggers. I eventually became a jogger because of them and participated in some races. I found this helped me when the stress was high. Many times, before I was to meet Greg, I took off for a quick run or a fast walk to clear the cobwebs and to get the endorphins going. At this time our children were with me for two weeks and their dad for two weeks. He had been commuting, dropping them off and picking them up, but after mediation I had to start picking them up on my two weeks and he would pick them up on his two weeks.

After he remarried he had his wife come and pick up the children once. I didn't say anything to her, but I told Greg if she ever came to my house again to pick up our children I would beat the crap out of her. She never came to the house again. I don't know why I said that. I hadn't gotten into a physical fight since junior high with a girl in my class. We were going out the door at the end of school when she made a remark that started the fight. We ended up on the ground in the grass and I was on top of her hitting her. I finally came to my senses and realized this was not the way to handle disagreements. I got up and walked away. After that I made a promise to myself that I would never get into a fight again. I could not call myself a Christian and behave that way.

~~~~~~~~~~

Mother's Day

It was Mother's Day and I wanted to send my mother flowers. I called her friend where mother was living to get her correct address.

She said, "She doesn't live here anymore. Didn't you

know, she moved back with your dad."

I didn't know. Mother didn't tell me about her plans to move in with our dad. I didn't even know they had been talking that often. I think she was embarrassed to say anything. When I was seven years old I had prayed and prayed for my mother and father to get back together, and now God was answering my prayers. It took almost forty years for this to happen. I told the Sunday school class I was teaching that sometimes it takes a long time for God to answer prayers. It didn't last long though. My dad was a real slob, he wasn't clean and neat like he once was and didn't want to do repairs on his place. I called her at my dad's and she was just coming in from work. As we were talking she saw things were missing and asked him where the television and stereo were. He had gone out and left the door unlocked. He lived next door to a halfway house for convicted criminals. They were on the lookout for when he left to take advantage of his absence. After they were robbed she decided to find a place that was safer. He didn't want to leave because he had such cheap rent since he did maintenance on the property for the owner. I know my dad's heart was broken. She left him again. I don't know why they thought they could get back together again like they were still in their 20s. Like the old saying, "there was too much water under the bridge." She put her name in for senior housing since Social Security was her only income. It took some time, but she was accepted in the program and moved into a tiny studio apartment. It was too small for her even. She had to sleep on the couch and when we came to stay there was no room for us to stay with her. She kept her name on the list for a one-bedroom apartment, but it was in a high crime area. She ended up moving there in spite of that and did not go out in the evening.

<hr/>

Sailing Club

When I went sailing I was never seasick or afraid of the water even though I didn't think I was a strong swimmer. I could tread water for a short period of time, but would probably drown if I fell overboard in rough seas. It was not easy to schedule sails on Saturday because everyone wanted that day. My sails were frequently scheduled when it was my weekend with my children. It was stressful if I sailed on Sunday when the kids were with their dad, as we always had to clean the boat before leaving. That meant I had to rush home in the Sunday afternoon traffic in order to be home when he was dropping them off.

I was so desperate for help I sent my sister and her husband a letter to see if they would be interested in helping me so I could drop them off on Friday and then sail on Saturday and come back home on Sunday to pick them up and drive to Walnut Creek. She never answered my letter.

Once when she was visiting me in Walnut Creek she said, "Brit, tell your dad that I would like to have you and Case to come and spend some time with me."

I could hardly contain myself. I was in the kitchen when I heard her say this. I came running out of the kitchen and asked her, "Why would you want to have them while Greg has them, but didn't want to have them when I needed your help?"

Her response was, "I want to have them when I want to, not when you want me to have them."

I didn't pursue the conversation. It was of no use to go into why, it was her decision not to help me in my most needy time.

I belonged to the sailing club for thirty years and was grateful to have this as a way to get myself back to normal. It was a time to be out in the fresh air, and give the mind some relief of all of the stress and chaos from the divorce and custody issues.

CHAPTER FIVE

Growing up in Washington, DC: *Trip to Troutdale*

When I was seven my dad and uncle took us to visit mother's family in Virginia. Mother said she couldn't make the trip due to her job but probably the real reason was she didn't want to make the trip. I found out years later the reason for her not going to see her mother for over twenty years. She planned on leaving our dad and taking us to grandma's, but was told by her mother, "You're married, your place is with your husband."

My mother's father was killed in the coal mines in West Virginia the day after her sixth birthday. It was supposed to be his last day working in the coal mines. He was the only one injured that day, and died from a head injury when the roof collapsed. My grandfather and grandmother bought a farm in Virginia and were returning to farming. My grandmother had one child nine months old, a four-year-old, my mother who was six, a nine, twelve, and a fourteen-year-old at home, and a seventeen and nineteen-year-old that were living close by. It was on her birthday when our mother had to deal with memories of his death. I often wondered how her life would have been different if her father lived and they moved as a family to Virginia. Was our grandmother bitter about what life had dealt her and she took her disappointments out on my mother? I know my mother had to quit school in second grade to take over the duties of the house of cleaning, cooking and laundry. Her brother, who was nine, helped her, but the older ones had to find work to help support the family. She told me that when she was eleven years old she wanted to be baptized and her mother wouldn't let her. It was a Lutheran church and I am not sure, but it might have been the church her mother didn't approve of. If she had a better home life would things have been different for my sisters and me?

I asked her, "What job did you always want when you were younger?"

She said, "I wanted to be a secretary."

I think when she was a waitress she saw all the young women coming into the restaurant where she worked who might have been secretaries and she wished she could have been in their shoes. She was good in math and read a lot, so if she attended a secretarial school I know she would have been able to achieve her dreams, but there was no one to encourage her. She was a hard worker and never went on welfare. My father told her she could earn more money as a waitress with tips and salary than at her job with the post office. That was her incentive to become a waitress.

The trip to our grandmother's was uneventful, but long. It was about eighteen hours. My dad fixed his old panel truck and put a mattress in the back so we could sleep when we got tired. I remember waking up and my sisters and I were in the truck parked outside of our grandmother's. It was early in the morning and there was no one around, they were all asleep.

I remember all of the women in the kitchen preparing dinner. It was August and the wood stove made it extremely hot. I saw them cleaning the chicken they just killed and there was no sink, just dish pans to use. They had to pump the water they needed for cleaning and cooking. I thought: I am so glad I am not an adult, and what hard work it was to fix a meal. The outhouse was a challenge for us, especially at night if we didn't want to use the chamber pot in the bedroom. I remember being afraid of the snakes as we walked to the outhouse at night, and my uncle holding the door for me. The house was over one-hundred years old and the outhouse was probably put in at that time. I realized when I was older why my mother never spoke of an interest to go camping with us. She grew up without the modern conveniences and didn't need to go camping to know what it was like to experience nature. I learned too late she always wanted to go to Disneyland.

The trip back home was different. The van was loaded with canned fruits and vegetables in glass jars from our family. That was the way they did things, sharing whatever they had. We were asleep and woke up to people pulling us out of the truck. My dad had been drinking and turned the truck over. The lucky thing was we turned over into the mountain. If we turned over on the steep outside of the mountain we probably would not have survived. The women in the group that stopped to help us took us to their car, making sure we were okay and comforting us. The men were able to turn the truck right side up and we were on our way back to Washington, DC. Once we were on the road again my dad continued to drink. At one time a fire started in the front on the floor and they just poured beer on it to put it out and kept on driving, not even stopping. When we got to the city the back doors of the truck flew open while we were going around one of the many circles for traffic. He wouldn't even stop to shut the doors. My uncle tried to get him to stop, but he kept going. It was amazing that no policemen were around at that time. When we finally got home, mother was not there. She moved out while we were gone. I guess that was her plan.

I remember her asking me before she moved, "How would I feel about having a new father?"

I don't think I could answer her. That was too big a decision to make.

Her big reason for leaving was his inability to keep a job. She planned on taking us with her after she was settled, but was not able to do so. My dad and his brother, who was a policeman at the time, told her they would make sure she would never get custody. They "would see to it that she would be destroyed in court" was their constant threat. My uncle divorced his wife and kept custody of my cousin, and she knew that they would do the same thing to her.

※※※※※※※※

Finding a Place for Us for the Summer

Previously, when both my parents worked we had African-American females to babysit. We had one we had grown fond of and missed her when she left for a better-paying job.

I don't know why my dad didn't look for another African-American female to come watch us, but he was looking for a place we could stay in the summer. We drove to see one place in the suburbs. We were in the car of our dad's friend, and I was in the front seat when I turned around to talk to my sisters. I saw the back car door was open and my sister Prip was gone. I looked back down the road and could see she was laying on the side of the road. We turned around and by then another car had stopped to come to her aid. It was a miracle she was okay, just cuts and bruises. Cars didn't go very fast in those days thankfully, but then the good Lord was looking out for us again. I don't know how else to explain how she was okay. When we got to the home my dad was considering for us, they washed her and attended to her cuts and scratches. As for going to a doctor, my dad was sure she was okay. We just had to hope he was right. The family he was considering for child care lived across the street from us on Meigs Place. They had moved, but I recognized the son. I used to follow him around the neighborhood and once went into his house when his mother and dad were there. I was sitting on the couch when his dad put his arm around me and put his hand inside my panties on my private parts. His wife was standing in the doorway of the living room and watching him. His son was standing on the other side of the room and could see what he was doing.

The wife told him, "What are you going to do if she tells her parents?"

He didn't seem worried. He probably thought no one

would believe me, since he was such an honorable person, a respected fireman. She did nothing. I don't remember how I got out of that situation. It was like I was trapped.

I told my mother and she said, "Don't you tell your dad. He will kill that man."

I never told anyone of that instance. I wondered if his son became a child molester after watching his dad. I never hung around the son after that. I knew if our dad left us there I would have had to keep watch over my sisters all the time, and that was really going to cause me more stress. Luckily our dad didn't want to leave us there. I don't know what was said or why, but another time to thank the good Lord for watching out for us.

<hr />

Poultry Farm, Virginia

It was then that he took my sisters and I to stay with a woman in Virginia who had a poultry farm, and took children into her home. When he left us there in the beginning he wouldn't let our mother know where we were. Finally, she was able to get on his good side and was able to visit us. The day he dropped us off and left we didn't cry. We thought it would be fun, a new adventure living in the country, but the next time he came to visit us reality set in, and we didn't want to stay.

We cried and begged, "Please take us with you," but he still left us there.

After summer was over we went back to Washington to live, but later because there was no one to watch us while he worked, he took us back to Virginia for the school year. By then I was in the third grade.

While we were staying there I was responsible for taking care of my sisters, the wife's son, and her nephew. In the evening I bathed everyone and got them in their pajamas, and then I was the last one to take a bath in the same water. Because we were on well water, we had to bathe this way. In the summertime we would bathe in a big galvanized tub outside. I cleaned the house, which was a three-bedroom, two-story house, washed the dishes after every meal, fed the ducks and chickens and carried pails of water to them. She would go behind me after I dusted or swept to show me what I missed, and if the dishes were not properly cleaned I would have to redo them. I helped her with the enormous amount of canning she did in the summer. We picked berries, peeled tomatoes, peaches, and apples for canning. When it was time to kill the chickens, I had to clean up the kitchen behind her. After that I couldn't stand to eat chicken. She made chicken salad sandwiches for my school lunch, but the sandwiches were awful. She left the skin on the boiled chicken and used a sandwich spread that didn't help the taste. Because she sold poultry and chickens to the neighbors, there were always chickens being killed. I also hung the wash by myself, bought it in, and folded the clothes. It was at this time I started walking in my sleep.

I remember the first instance—coming downstairs to the kitchen, fixing the coffee and putting it on the burner. I set the table for breakfast and then tried to open the door to get out. I wasn't totally awake so I couldn't figure out how to open the door. When I looked out the window and it was dark outside, I couldn't understand why. Then I realized it was not morning. Not one person in the house heard me. So, I put everything back and went back to bed.

Our dad usually came to pick us up every other weekend and then drove us back on Sunday night or early Monday morning. I had made up my mind my sisters and I were going to hitchhike back to Washington. I knew that if I could get up in the middle of the night, make all the noise I did when I was sleep walking and no one woke up, then we should be able to escape. We would be a good way down the road before anyone would find us missing. We had driven those roads so many times I knew by heart the way to get back home. I don't know why my dad finally decided to come and take us back home. He probably owed her money. He more than likely figured that since I was working like an adult she was getting all the payment she deserved. It was fate because I was ready to make the escape. I knew again the good Lord was taking care of us. There was nothing that was going to make me change my mind. I was only eight years old then, my sisters were five and four, but I was sure we could make the trip. We walked all over Washington when we were at home. I don't know how they were able to keep up with me, but they did. If my dad hadn't come to get us, we were going to get back to Washington on our own.

Since I was the oldest I was left to babysit them and took care of them when our parents were not available. I never resented taking care of them. I loved them as much as our parents did. I did get frustrated when they would not do what I told them to do since I was their substitute parent.

We went back to Meigs Place in Washington, DC with our dad, but shortly after that we moved to East Capitol Street. My dad wanted to get away from the neighbors who were always asking about our situation and where our mother had moved to. He was worried that the neighbors would call child welfare because he left us on our own so much.

We found out then that mother made plans to move to Germany with her husband, who was stationed there with the Army, and had already left with his group. She wanted to take us, but our dad wouldn't let her. My dad used her husband's absence to try to woo her back. She would stay at our house during the day, and we would go to her apartment for the night. They were like husband and wife again.

The next time she came back to our house they had been drinking and dad was moving her into the house with all of her belongings. They were going to get back together again. Sometime later I saw her as she watched him go across the street to the drug store where a former girlfriend, Ro, worked. Mother went across the street to the park where she could see into the drug store and saw them talking. I guess it was then that she decided not to stay. He promised he would not be seeing Ro anymore, but argued "how could he not run into her?" She lived only two doors away from us, and her daughter Jo and I were friends. My sisters and I went to church with Jo, and we were in the same classroom in junior high. We thought our dad and Ro were going to get married at one time, and had high hopes that this would make us a happy family again.

After, Ro started saying disparaging things about mother, "I told him if he married her that I would not live with them."

I don't think that had anything to do with his decision, because he always did what was good for him. That was when mother again made plans to go to Germany to join her husband. I don't remember her ever telling us when she was leaving. I remember her packing and getting ready, but didn't know the day, until I came home from school for lunch and found the note on the table from her. I don't remember crying, I think I was in shock. I went back to school but I guess the tears came later. It was an empty feeling when she left and we were on our own again. I think when she was there it lifted a heavy burden from my shoulders. I don't think we wanted to cry in front of our dad because we were worried about hurting his feelings, so we just picked up and started back into our regular routine.

After East Capitol street we moved to 12th Place. The rent was cheaper, and my dad was having problems buying coal on a regular basis and that was our only source of heat. If he didn't put the order in before we ran out it meant no heat and we all had to sleep in one bed with our warmest clothes on. There were times when the gas was turned off, and thankfully we could cook on the waffle iron which had a flat side for grilling sandwiches. Other times the electricity was turned off and that would mean getting the candles and flashlight out. He planned on renting out rooms, but that didn't happen. He started fixing the rooms up, but was never able to complete the job.

At 12th Place we were in a "shotgun house," where you could see from the front door through to the two bedrooms, the kitchen and out to the back yard. We had coal heat at this house also, so ordering coal before we ran out was important. One thing about this house since it was on one floor and small we could always turn on the gas oven for heat. It was not the nicest place to live. There were no trees, no grass or shrubs, just concrete. There was a school across the street from us and there was no grass there either. Both sides of the street were all concrete. There were a lot of kids playing outside and people would sit on their front concrete steps in the day and evening. We made friends with two sisters who lived a couple of doors down from us. They were really bad off, as they didn't have any furniture. I took them to church several times and even lent them some of my clothes, since they didn't have church clothes. Their lives were very different than ours. In fact, our dad said if we didn't stop playing with them he would send us back to Virginia. I don't know why he thought they were a bad influence on us. I never told him of anything we did, but one time they talked me into going into the supermarket and stealing something. They had been in a girl gang where they lived, and that's what the gangs did to new recruits, to prove you would fit in. I went into the store and stole a bottle of olives since they were my favorite thing to eat, and we only had them at holidays. I felt so bad for the store owners and had such a guilty conscience for stealing that I never did that again. I knew stealing was wrong and always considered myself a Christian. I was trying to show them a better way to live and all I was accomplishing was letting them bring me down to their standards.

When my sisters and I wanted money to buy candy we would collect soda bottles and turn them in to buy penny candy. I used my wagon to go to the grocery store and haul groceries for the women shoppers. I was the only girl and the only Caucasian, so I think I was able to get more jobs this way. The youngest sister had a different way to earn money. She knew someone in the neighborhood she would go to and he would give her twenty-five or fifty cents to let him touch her private parts. She eventually was picked up in a bar by the police, where she would go and sing for money from the patrons. She was sent to reform school after that, but when she came home for a short visit she had new clothes and shoes, so it didn't seem so bad to her. The food was more regular than what she had at home which added to her positive opinion of her stay.

Later at 12th Place when I wanted money for anything I went door-to-door looking for jobs cleaning house. One of the first jobs I had was cleaning for an African-American family. I think she hired me because she wanted to help me out since her house was already so clean. That was evident when she had me clean her bathroom and even that was very clean. Another time I cleaned her wood venetian blinds with a special liquid she supplied. I never told my dad, as I am sure he would have been very mad especially since, I am ashamed to say, his family in North Carolina had slaves on their farm. When we drove to California we met one of the ancestors that was still with the family. My dad and my uncle would talk about Pho all the time, amazed that she was still working for the family.

The sisters and their family moved shortly after that, and I made friends with two African-American sisters. They had higher standards than the Caucasian sisters.

They had an older brother who seemed like he wanted to challenge me to a fight. He kept walking into me and bumping against me.

I finally challenged him, telling him, "I will fight you if that's what it takes, but you are going to leave me alone."

He was much taller and older than me. I don't know where I found the nerve to do that. I had never done that before. Many years later someone told me that he probably had a crush on me, and that is one of the ways boys get attention from girls, since they are too shy to start up a conversation. I think he thought since I was friends with his sisters that we could be friends also. In those days it was unusual for Caucasian girls to be friends with African-American boys. I was in sixth grade and eleven years old, and I think he must have been a couple of years older, since he was so much taller than me. Integration in schools didn't start until I was in junior high school. I remember how big his eyes became, and how he was looking up to the sky and didn't say a thing. I don't know if anyone else heard what I said to him, but after that he left me alone.

While we were living there I had another instance of sleep walking. My sisters and I had fallen asleep on the couch and I woke up and saw a man in my dad's bedroom tearing everything up looking for something. I saw him taking the sheets and covers off his bed. I very quietly woke up my sisters, and told them we had to run outside because there was a man in our dad's bedroom. We all got up at the same time and ran out the door which was only a few steps from the couch. It was very late and there were no lights in any of the windows in the neighborhood. I didn't want to wake up any of my neighbors since they would know we had been left alone. I knew I had to go around to the alley and look in the window in my dad's bedroom to see if he was still there, but was too afraid to move. I don't know how long we stood outside until I finally was able to get the courage to go down the alley to look in the window. When I did, to my amazement there was nothing disturbed in his room.

I don't remember if this was the time when he didn't come home for three nights, which might explain the reason for me having this nightmare. We went to school for the three days and scrounged for food in the cabinets and refrigerator. Since I was the cook I tried to find things for our meals as best I could. There was nothing else we could do. We didn't have a telephone, but who would I have called? My dad's brother came by and wanted to know where our dad was and I told him I hadn't seen him for three days. He left without any offer of help. When my dad showed up I found out he had been to Ro's house. I don't know if that was where he was for the entire time, since he didn't think he needed to give us an explanation.

When we were living there I fell at school when I tripped on a ripple in the floor. I was taken by ambulance to Casualty Hospital as I had broken my arm. When I was in the emergency room they tried to pull my arm back into place. Jo was outside the room and heard me pleading with them to please stop. It seemed like it went on forever, but they finally realized they were not going to be able to fix my arm that way. I don't know how they got hold of my dad since we didn't have a phone. They asked me if we had insurance and I told them the name of the insurance company, but the policy did not cover medical issues. It was for burial expenses. I remember the insurance man coming by for payment on a regular basis. The hospital wouldn't operate on me because we didn't have insurance, so I laid in the bed in pain the rest of the day, that night, and part of the next day before they operated on me. I don't know what my dad had to do to get them to operate, because I knew we didn't have money to pay the bill.

After I was released and went home it was very depressing. I said something at the dinner table about the chicken not being done, as it was still bloody, and he exploded. I think he might have been drinking because of the stress of no money. He could have bought school insurance for fifty cents for the school year, but didn't believe in insurance, except for burial. He said his family never went to doctors or hospitals in their lifetime, feeling that most health problems could be healed at home. He often talked about him getting shot in the foot and never going to the doctor. At other times he would give us kerosene and sugar to heal us for whooping cough. Instead he bought burial insurance for all of us. That was the way some of the country people felt. You need to have money to be buried.

After that we moved to 11th street, where our family friends Clyde and Thelma lived. I don't know why our dad decided to move there, but it was a nicer home with grass in the front and back.

There were two African-American sisters on both sides of our home that became our good friends. I went over to check on my sisters, and they were curling Prip's hair with their curling iron that they put on the stove to heat up. I had never seen anyone curl a Caucasian's hair with a curling iron that African-Americans used. I didn't know what to say. I was afraid they were going to burn her hair off, but my sister didn't seem to mind. She was only eight years old and I am sure she liked the attention. I always fixed her and Lynn's hair in the morning before school and when we went to church. I thought I did a good job, using barrettes and ribbons, trying different styles and even cutting their hair which didn't always turn out well. In fact, I had cut my hair, but really made a mess. My Confirmation was the next day and I was trying to find a beauty salon in the area that could take me for a quick haircut. The four sisters went with me down to H Street and we shopped for a haircut. We went into several African-American shops and they asked if anyone had time to cut my hair. The look the salon workers gave us made me realize they probably thought we were really dumb to come into their shop and ask for a haircut for me. I knew they would not be able to cut the hair of a Caucasian, but I didn't want to say anything since our friends were trying to be helpful. I think at that time there were probably rules against any African-American shop cutting the hair of a Caucasian. I don't think the sisters realized there would be a problem. As it turned out I could find no one to give me a haircut, and I bought a hat to wear for my Confirmation. My haircut looked better as it grew out, but I didn't have good scissors or the knowledge for cutting hair.

While we lived there I gave a birthday party for my two sisters. Since their birthdays were only ten days apart it wasn't unusual to combine their parties, as there was only a year's difference in their age. They were what some people call "Irish twins." When the parents came with their children I could see the surprise on their face. I was only twelve at the time, but wore my Sunday dress with my pumps so I would appear more mature. We played party games out in the yard, and had cake and ice cream. Our budget was small, so there was not much in prizes. I could tell all were having a good time, and everyone was happy. I asked my sister Lynn what the best birthday party she had in her sixty-five years, and she said it was that party. I never knew that. It was the kind of birthday party I always wanted as a child.

It had been two years since mother left. The day she returned, my sisters met Jo and I as we were coming home from school and said, "Mother is back."

I couldn't believe it, we hadn't received any letters from her telling us when she was returning. I ran home and there she was on the porch with my dad and uncle. I threw down my books and wrapped my arms around her and cried into her shoulder. It was very emotional. I don't think my dad realized how much I missed her and how much I loved her until then. I think they shed a few tears also.

A few months later her husband went back to Germany again, and she didn't want to return with him. I think it was too hard for her to leave us again. I found out later that our aunt had seen him come out of the house of a former girlfriend, so this resulted in her divorcing him for being unfaithful. I don't know if he confessed or she just went ahead and divorced him to get back and hurt him, as his actions hurt her. It was then that our dad finally let us go live with her. She found an apartment in Georgetown and bought new furniture for the apartment. It was a nice place to live, but I commuted back to the old neighborhood to attend my school since I was close to graduating from ninth grade. I am not sure what our dad's plan was when he let us live with our mother. He and my uncle made a couple of trips to California. So, us being with mother meant he didn't have to make living arrangements for us while he was gone.

<hr/>

Moving to California

Our dad usually came to mother's to pick us up and do things with us, mainly visiting his brother and his family. We had been with mother for several months, when one day he asked us how would we like to move to California. Had this been his plan all along when he let us live with mother? I never thought to ask him about that, but he might not have been truthful. We thought moving to California sounded like fun, especially after seeing Disneyland on the television. He told us not to say anything to our mother. He would tell us when we were going. He told me he would pick us up while mother was at work and not to say anything. She wouldn't be home until after 2:00 a.m. since she worked as a waitress. We packed our things and left a note for her that we had gone to California with our dad. I know we probably broke her heart. This was not something she was expecting. She never talked about it, but I feel bad that I was responsible for hurting her so deeply.

All the way down the road they thought the police would be after them for taking us. When we got to North Carolina and were staying with relatives I think they finally realized she hadn't called the police about him taking us. Since she didn't have custody there was probably nothing legally she could do. When we arrived in California we were excited to see all the palm trees and orange groves.

We were in the car with my uncle and Lynn had been annoying our uncle with her feet under his seat. He told her not to do it again, and the next time she did it, he pulled the car over of on the side of the freeway, he turned around and gave her a vicious slap across the face. He was a bully, not a good person. He didn't treat his daughter that way. He did the same thing to me once, when he came into the kitchen and he saw water on the table by his vodka. He thought I poured his vodka out in the sink and that was why there was water on the table. He came into our bedroom and hit me across the face. I started to leave the house, but he stopped me. He probably knew I was going to go to the police which was why he wouldn't let me leave the house. Our dad wasn't home when this happened, but they later had a discussion about this episode. Since our uncle was paying most of the bills there wasn't much he could do. Not long after that our uncle moved with his family into a housing development for low income families and we followed sometime later.

It didn't get much better after that as my dad had a difficult time getting a job since he wouldn't join the union. He was a carpenter and had never been part of a union. I don't know if being from the South made him think that way, but most jobs required joining the union. My uncle told me once if I went to the authorities and told them how things are with our dad not working, not having food in the house, or clothes when we needed them, they would probably send me and my sisters back to mother. I don't think he was thinking of us, just that he was probably tired of supporting all of us. We called mother collect when we were all living together, but since we didn't have a phone now we couldn't contact her to tell her how things were.

My dad said that his brother owed him. I am not sure what he was referring to, but there was a lumber business they were part of with another partner that mysteriously burned down. My mother's brother and I thought dad might have been responsible for the fire, since we both knew he was out the night of the incident. I also saw a letter he started to write beginning with the words, "To whom it may concern." As part of the business dad and the other partner had built a house, but were not able to sell it for their costs. That might have been the reason for the fire. Whose idea was to burn the business down? One of the business owners next to them thought it was my uncle who he referred to as the "crooked cop." My cousin might have picked up some of the same ethics from his dad when he told me I would be able to sell more of the pot holders I made if I told people my sister was in the hospital and we needed money for her care. I took his suggestions and went out of my neighborhood to sell my potholders. I didn't realize someone recognized me, and asked my dad about our sister who was in the hospital. He asked me why I telling people my sister was in the hospital. That was the only time I did that. A good way to learn a lesson about ethics.

I came home from school one day when out of the blue my sisters told me we were going to be moving. I got very upset at this news. It hadn't been easy getting adjusted in new schools and making friends. I couldn't find anything about this move to be positive. I decided I was not going to be moving. I called a friend to give me a ride to see a lady I babysat for to see if I could stay with her and babysit on a regular basis. She was agreeable, so this would work out for both of us, since she had two young boys and I would go to school in the day and babysit in the evening. When I came home it was late and my dad had been drinking. I was always home, so it was unusual for me not to be there when he came home. I didn't tell him my plans, just went into the bedroom I shared with my younger sister. He followed me and started attacking me, and I was defending myself. Lynn was in the bed watching us not knowing what to do. He was on top of me on the floor and was choking me. I thought okay, I am going to die and quit fighting back, then he quit attacking me. He didn't say anything about being sorry for his abuse then or the next day before I left for school.

I told a friend about the attack and showed her the bruises and scratches. I wasn't sure if I wanted to go home, or what was waiting for me. I went home with my friend and her mother didn't know how to advise me, but said there was a police officer down the street and he could probably help me. If I wanted her to she would call him. We went to his house and he said I should go to the station and start the process with a complaint against my dad. He said that the legal system would send me to a cottage where they sent children and young people in these situations. I didn't know what to do so I called my mother to see what she thought I should do. She thought it would be best to go to the police station and make the complaint. I thought this would be best for my sisters and me. This would be a way for all three of us to get back to our mother.

When all of the paperwork was complete and I was taken to the cottage called McLaren Hall there was another big shock. It wasn't a cottage, it was an institution. It seemed all of the children in this facility were held while the courts made the decision about their lives. I was never examined before by a doctor. I didn't know what to expect. The other girls told me they did this on all females to see if you were pregnant or sexually active. It was extremely painful for me since I was still a virgin. That night we were in a group singing and being entertained since there was no television. I just sat there and started crying and couldn't stop. This wasn't unusual behavior for new people. They all knew what I was going through. I was assigned my own room which was bare, just a bed and mattress, no lights to read by at night as all lights were turned out when each person went in their room. The door had a window so that they could check on the individuals. I don't know if this was normal to have my own room, but I was glad I didn't have to share with someone I might not like. At night I would stand in front of the window and look at all the lights of the city of Los Angeles and sing. I sang all the songs I knew from church and the popular songs of that year, 1958. My sisters and

I always liked to pretend to be the Lennon Sisters when we sang together. I think we sounded good for amateurs. I loved to sing and always volunteered in singing groups at church and school.

When I was assigned a social worker the most important thing was that I wanted to know about my sisters. She told me they had moved to Tulare. My dad had been arrested after my complaint and there would be a trial. After that I probably would be sent back to my mother, and she would have to start a case on child custody for my sisters.

I kept asking my social worker when I would be able to return to school. There were still a few weeks left for the school term. She told me they were able to find a place for me at a Catholic girl's school in the San Gabriel Valley area. I did not know any area except for San Pedro where we lived and Long Beach. The name of the school was Maryvale. Before I left McLaren Hall, I asked for a Bible from the counselors. Some individuals had a Bible placed in their room by the Gideon Group, a religious organization, but mine didn't have one. One boy I made friends with gave me his and on the inside inscribed *love, GM*. I kept that Bible for over fifty years. It was hard to let it go in my garage sale. I saw one woman reading the inscription and I almost took it back. I thought about going on Facebook to track him down to see if he was still alive. He promised to look out for my sisters if they should be put in McLaren Hall after I left.

As it was, there was no rooms in the dormitory at Maryvale, so I was given a room in the hospital area with Sister Esther. I had my own room again which was nice.

She was very calming and very concerned about my situation. It was a good fit for me. She was like the grandmother I didn't have growing up. Sister Aurelia worked in the dormitory where the other girls my age were assigned. She was younger and was another special person that was a big help to me, just because of her friendship and concern. Since I was not Catholic I went to church off campus. There were several social events with the boys in the Catholic school in the area. It seemed that most of these boys were going into the seminary after graduating from high school. I didn't have clothes for school and tried to sew some outfits and find clothing that had been left behind by others in the school. From what I learned of the other girls most of them were placed in the school because of problems in their family.

At the trial for my dad he told the judge that the bruises and cuts I had were from sports, basketball and baseball. I didn't play either of these sports. It wasn't pleasant seeing him. I remember shouting at him that he wouldn't be able to keep my sisters after this. He paid no attention and left.

My friend's mother from high school in San Pedro offered to take me in if there was no suitable place for me to live with my family. The social worker determined that since I wanted to go back to live with my mother that would be best for me. I did stay with them for a visit while travel arrangements were made. Her concern for me was very touching and she wrote to me several times, but other things got in the way of regular letters between us.

My social worker told me that my mother had remarried. I said, "Oh, yes and we like our stepfather." I thought she was talking about her first husband after my dad.

When I arrived back at my mother's apartment she introduced her new husband. I was tired and somewhat shocked when she introduced me to her new husband, and I asked her why she remarried. I know that wasn't very nice of me, but I had been traveling for a long time. I missed my plane, as my friends didn't know how long it would take to get to the airport in Los Angeles, and had to take a later flight. I cried for a couple of hours when I was on the plane until I was exhausted and fell asleep. It was a shock to me when I thought it was going to be just her and me, but I got over it and we got along fine. I know she was probably very depressed when we left and needed companionship. Getting married was one way to find the love she needed.

After getting settled the plan was for us to get a larger apartment so she could start the process of getting custody of my sisters. We were in a two-room apartment with a small kitchen and bathroom. I was given the bedroom and they used a roll-a-way bed they brought out in the evening. Her husband worked at a gas station, and he usually worked until late at night. When he came home he wanted to relax and watch television. So that worked best for them. He was a good-natured person and very likable, but together they both drank a lot and got into arguments that caused a lot of damage to the apartment. I sometimes came home from school or my part-time job and things were in shambles because of their drinking. I would go to my best friend's home to escape. We were both in the same classes and homeroom and were like the Bobbsey Twins, except she was petite and blond and

I was taller and had dark brown hair. Otherwise, I had no place to go. I found a job during Christmas and used the money to buy my clothes and for school expenses. I opened a savings account and put most of my money in an account to go back to California and bring my sisters back. I was very frugal with my money.

<hr/>

Quitting School

In my junior year in high school I worked evenings and weekends and then in the summer I worked forty-plus hours between two jobs. I received information from Western High School before my senior year that I would not be graduating with my class. I attended five schools in three years, and I was short of credits because they would not accept my classes from California.

During the summer I was offered a full-time position at the stock brokerage firm where I was working part-time for one of the brokers. The secretary decided to quit due to the pressure of the work. After finding out I wouldn't be graduating on time I decided to withdraw from school during the day and continue my education at night school for my high school diploma. My plan was to go to college eventually. I just didn't know how I was going to pay for it. No one in the office knew that I was only sixteen or that I hadn't graduated from high school. They thought the prom I went to was my prom, but it was my boyfriend's from eighth grade, as he was a year ahead of me. I think my maturity was due to being responsible for my sisters for so many years. When I look at pictures of myself from elementary school I looked like an old lady, a refugee from a labor camp. After my parents' divorce we were on our own so much I had the make many decisions about our care and safety. My dad would constantly tell me to stop worrying, let him do the worrying, but I couldn't stop worrying. While working I saved my money. I was able to work a great deal of overtime, since my job was my life, and I was the only secretarial help. I felt this job was a substitute for my family. I was needed and would stay until the job was finished since confirmations for trades had to go out immediately.

I moved out of my mother's apartment just down the hall from her in an efficiency apartment. I couldn't stand being around the drinking and fighting, and she was okay with my decision since I would be paying my own rent and I was still close by. Later, when my salary was increased I looked for a larger apartment so mother could start the custody case for my sisters. My mother and her husband did not want to move into a two-bedroom apartment because of the expense, so I took a one-bedroom apartment with the goal of going to California to bring my sisters back.

Because I worked for a brokerage firm I received some stock in the company as a bonus. I sold the stock, and with my savings I was able to fly to California to see my sisters. I didn't know where they lived so as I was walking I flagged down a police car and asked where the junior high school was. He gave me a ride to the school, otherwise I would have been walking a long time in the heat. I asked the school office to see my sister Lynn and went to her classroom. When I went into the room she was in the front row and didn't even recognize me. When I said her name, she got up from her seat and we stood in the classroom crying and embracing one another. The teacher didn't say anything, but we finally were able to stop crying and leave the classroom. I don't know what the other classmates thought was going on, but it was very emotional for us. From there we went to Prip's school and it was a big surprise to her also. We did a lot of visiting and just staying around town because they were both still in school. I was staying in a hotel downtown since I didn't feel comfortable at their home. When it was time to leave them, I said good-bye and took the Greyhound Bus for a long ride back to Los Angeles for my flight. I cried all the way to Los Angeles. When I arrived in Los Angeles I could not leave them. I turned around and took the next bus back to Tulare, where they lived. After visiting again, I said goodbye and took the bus back to Los Angeles for my flight. I couldn't leave them, and again I turned around and went back to Tulare. My heart was breaking. I couldn't go back to Washington without them, but I couldn't stay. I had a job to go back to that I didn't have in Tulare. This time we just started packing their things and for some reason our dad didn't object. He even drove us back to Los Angeles to catch the flight back to Washington. I had to call my boss and borrow the money for their airfare. He knew how much they meant to me. I wondered if he was worried about how I was going to be able to pay him back, but he never voiced a concern. As it was I did pay him back. I found with the extra expense of my sisters it was not as easy to pay rent, buy groceries and pay school expenses for them. In addition, there were expenses for eyeglasses for my middle sister and dental visits. I found a second job and worked evenings and weekends at a department store in order to buy them clothes and Christmas presents. They were still in junior high school, but no one ever questioned my age or asked for any guardianship papers.

I allowed them to have some friends over for a birthday party since their birthday was only ten days apart. The janitor gave us his permission to use one of the basement rooms for the party. I bought all the food, sodas, and cake for them. I was working in the evening and was planning on being at the party before it broke up. As I was walking down the street from Connecticut Avenue I saw groups of young people walking up the street. Some were staggering and helping others and then I started running to where the party was. I found out there had been drinking and the young men started to jump the janitor and were going to beat him up. I took my sisters back to the apartment and we turned out the lights and sat quietly. Someone called the police and I didn't want them to question my age or where our parents were. We heard someone come to the door and knock, but we stayed still until they left. I apologized to the janitor and felt bad about him being attacked because I wasn't there to supervise the party. Things had changed since I was in junior high school. I never experienced this type of behavior at a birthday party.

My mother was surprised that my dad let them go so easily. I think he was ready for a vacation from the financial obligations. She thought he sent them back to live with her, but because of her and her husband's drinking, they did not want to live with her. I worked and supported us for almost a year with no help from either of my parents. Life with my dad and his wife was unbearable at times due to their problem with alcohol. They lived in poverty because of his drinking and his lack of motivation to hold a job to take care of his family.

They wanted to go back to California because they missed their friends. Lynn was not happy with me being the boss, and Prip usually went along with her. I was going to move back to mother's and pay off the bills I had accumulated while taking care of them. Then I would save my money and move back to Los Angeles and look for a job there and they could join me then if they wanted. Instead I met and married the father of my two older children. I am sure many times they wished they stayed with me, as things just got worse for them. Prip ended up getting married while she was still in high school. Lynn and I think she married for her husband's family. He was such a good person and his family loved her and would do anything for the both of them. She left the marriage after a few years, not sure that she really loved him like a wife should love her husband. I think they were going through a stage in their marriage and if they received counseling they might have made a happy marriage.

CHAPTER SIX

Tea Dances and Dating JW

I heard friends talking about the tea dances at the Hyatt on Fridays in downtown San Francisco and they sounded like fun. It took some time for me to work up the nerve to go since I was by myself. It was at 5:30 p.m. so it was easy to go right after work when I didn't have our children. It was a walk of seven blocks to the Hyatt, and it was at one of my first tea dances that I met JW. He was tall, had nice blue eyes, beautiful premature silver hair, very good looking, and he dressed impeccably. I knew that I wanted to know him better. He asked for my phone number, but then didn't call for several weeks. I didn't see him at the tea dances for some time after that, but I was always looking for him. Then some weeks later he showed up again and we started going out. I had been working on healing myself and trying to not let the divorce and custody issues affect my mental and physical health. I knew he was a man of quality and I didn't want him to think of me as another screwed-up divorcee. It was so wonderful to have adult companionship, to go out to dinner to nice restaurants, and it was a good feeling to finally have someone so nice to care about me. The first time he came to the house to meet Brit and Case he brought me flowers and a small bouquet for Brit and she just glowed. He really knew how to get to my heart and hers by bringing her flowers to make her smile again. It was hard to juggle dating and taking care of Brit and Case, and most of the time I didn't date when they were with me. JW seemed to really enjoy them. They brought smiles to everyone. I always thought they were better than television to watch. He knew of the problems I had with my neighbors and the homeowners' association complaining about my roommates. I received letters on a regular basis about my property, complaining about weeds in the front yard, the grass needing to be cut, or that I had left my trash cans out in front of the house too long.

He came to Brit's birthday party, and I was able to talk Bett into dressing up as a clown for entertainment.

She asked, "Do I have to talk?"

I said, "No, you don't have to talk."

She was a great clown, Brit was the happiest I had ever seen her and all of the kids had a great time chasing Bett all over the house and out to the yard. We had face painting and since the weather was still warm I was able to have the party outside on the deck. If only that happy feeling could have lasted forever.

After that I was looking for another roommate and I had a response from a man from El Salvador who wanted to rent the room for him and his family. He would do yard work and handy man jobs for me while his wife would take care of my children. I wasn't sure if this was going to work for me, because then I wouldn't have the extra income which would make it difficult to meet my expenses. Another concern was if I rented to this family would their friends and family be dropping by and visiting often? He was very persuasive and kept finding a solution every time I said, "but what about?" I thought this might be the answer to my childcare problems. I would not have to drag Brit and Case out in the wee hours of the morning, and rush to meet my van pool. In the evening, I would have more energy since I didn't have to stop and pick them up. I made the mistake of talking to JW about this family and he thought it was a bad idea. He convinced me that it wouldn't work, so I didn't even give them a try. I usually went on my gut feeling about new roommates. I gave it a lot of thought and prayed a great deal also. I generally didn't ask for advice from anyone. I later thought maybe I made a mistake by letting him talk me out of giving them a try.

One instance where I used my gut feeling and instinct was when I interviewed an individual while Case and Brit were in the room. The man had blue eyes that were very unusual.

After he left, Case, who was only three at the time said, "You aren't going to rent to that man with the werewolf eyes are you mom?"

I told him no, but it was amazing how this little kid could look at someone's eyes and get bad vibes also.

JW came to my house when I was having the sailing club over for an afternoon pool party. I woke up sick the day of the party with the flu, and could not raise my head off the bed. Instead of him staying to help me through the sickness, he left thinking I would be better off on my own to deal with being sick and with my children. He didn't see that I needed help, all he knew was that he couldn't handle things when they were difficult.

He later decided that there was too much drama going on in my life for him. I was shocked, but thought maybe when he saw how difficult it was for me he might have felt guilty about leaving his family. He never talked about them, so I wasn't sure if he ever saw them.

Later when I rented my house and moved into an apartment in San Francisco he wanted to get back together again, but by then it was too late. I was interested in someone else. He dyed his hair a dark reddish brown and it was not flattering on him. He probably wanted to date much younger women and thought this would help him. It's too bad he didn't realize how attractive he was with his natural silver hair.

~~~~~~~~~

Roommate: *Bo #2*

I decided to place another ad for a roommate, since I realized that this was a way to have extra income and stay in my house. Bo called and said he was unemployed, that he had been laid off, but had just sold his house so he would be able to pay me rent. He also had a fifteen-year-old son. I decided to give him a chance, as I was to take over the house as my part of the property settlement since the house hadn't sold after nine months on the market. Interest rates were still high and people were not able to qualify for loans. The house payment was more than my take home pay so I needed to have room-mates. Bo and his son took the room with my furniture and stored their furniture. He put a lot of time into looking for a new job. After school was out for the summer his son went to visit his mother. He was continually calling his dad asking, "When are you going to bring me back to California?" I think Bo decided he was not going to bring him back. When his dad was napping the son would go upstairs to their bedroom and ask him when was he going to fix him something to eat. He was in high school and almost sixteen years old, but didn't seem to be able to make himself a sandwich. When Bo first moved in I felt he wanted to start a relationship with me. He was an attractive man, but I did not find him appealing romantically. Something just didn't click. Maybe after living with someone and seeing their flaws it ruins the romantic part. We did rent movies together and order pizza occasionally, and he helped me with various projects on the house. He helped me put coating on the windows upstairs to cut down on the heat in the summer. His son would vacuum occasionally which helped out, but my daughter Bett remarked to him that no matter how good he vacuumed it was probably not going to be good enough for me. I never realized I was such a perfectionist. At times we did have somewhat of a family feeling. He seemed to like Bett, Brit, and Case, and playing with them, calling my son "Dude" and joking with them.

I was active in the singles group and invited some of the group over for a barbeque and Bo came downstairs with no shirt and no shoes, in a very relaxed and casual way. He had been drinking, and I think he was feeling sorry for himself since he was still looking for work. After the group left I let him know I did not like his behavior. He was trying to make these people think there was something between us.

One weekend when Bo was supposed to be away, I brought JW over for a barbeque on Saturday. I spent Friday night at his apartment in San Francisco after we went out for dinner, and Saturday we decided to go to my house in Walnut Creek where it was warmer and we could lay out by the pool. Saturday night JW took me out to dinner again at a fancy restaurant in Walnut Creek and spent the night. I could tell Bo was not pleased that JW was there. I didn't feel comfortable with Bo at home while JW was there, but I decided to try and ignore his presence. After JW left Bo said, "We had an agreement, no overnight guests." I told him my agreement with him was that he was not to have overnight guests of the opposite sex. He could go to their place if he met someone. I fully expected all of my roommates would not to be at home so that no one would feel uncomfortable. Bo had recently taken a job in San Jose. I know he had not been feeling good about being out of work for so long and was anxious to be employed. His commute began early in the morning before 5:30 a.m., and not returning until after 7:00 p.m. The next week he left on Saturday morning not saying anything, not giving me any notice. I had been lenient and let him and his son move in without taking the last month's rent. I saw he packed his suitcase, but I thought he was going to be away for the weekend. He called me later in the week to let me know he would not be returning and wanting his security deposit returned. I told him he was not a very ethical person. I had let him and his son move in when he didn't have a job when others wouldn't take a chance on him. I gave them a room at the price for one person, not two, which I should not have done. So much for being sympathetic to his situation. I returned his deposit and just let it go, thinking that his reward would catch up with him eventually.

Shar: *Daycare*

Shar had a daycare center in her home and I had taken Brit there several times when I was showing property, and had somewhat of a regular schedule. She was recommended to me by the Contra Costa County child care license agency. She had a very large yard, but the pool had been covered over with dirt because of the safety hazard for the children. Her family and living room were taken over by the children in her care. In addition to her five children she was caring for several others. I could never be sure how many children were in her care because there were always so much activity going on. She knew I had the amniocentesis procedure before Brit and Case were born and called me with several questions since she was pregnant and her doctor recommended she have the procedure to prepare mentally if her child had any problems. She had the help of her two older children who were in high school in addition to other part-time help. I thought she would be able to provide a safe place for Brit and Case, and they would enjoy all of the other children to play with.

After Bett went to work for the bank I called Shar to see if she had space available at her daycare. She was the only person I found who would take them. It was a grueling schedule for both of my children to get up at 5:30 a.m. I had to drop them off in order to meet the carpool at 6:30. If we missed the carpool then we had to take BART, and that was a double expense, plus parking took extra time looking for available space. Sometimes when I arrived Shar was still in bed and it was dark and cold and I had to stand outside and keep knocking until someone came to the door. It was hard leaving them as I wasn't sure when I left them if she was going to watch them or go back to bed. One evening when I came to pick them up Case was in the highchair eating. One of the children said, "You know he has been in that highchair all day long."

I was worried they were just feeding him thinking this was the best way to keep him happy. He was almost nine pounds when he born, so he was a big baby. When my mother was with me she would get up and give him a bottle, then I would get up and give him a bottle and then Sy would get up and give him a bottle, so he was getting more than he needed in bottles. None of us realized the other was getting up with him, but he seemed to be thriving.

I always felt guilty leaving them at the sitter when I went to work, until I dropped Case off on a Saturday to take Brit to see the play *Annie* for her birthday. I didn't think he would be too happy about that since he wasn't going with us. As I was getting him settled and he started playing with the other children, Brit decided she wanted to stay and play with the other children. She didn't want to leave and go to the play. I almost had drag her out to the car, and then she cried, kicked, and screamed all the way to the theatre. This was one of those times I wanted to give up trying to make her happy. She was still having a difficult time with the divorce and separation. When we got to the theatre, I had to again almost drag her down the street. She kept saying, "I won't listen, I'll close my eyes and my ears." Finally, as we got closer to the theatre she saw the children who were in the play in their costumes, and then her face changed and I saw she was immediately more interested. I wanted to make sure she would have a good view, so I purchased front row seats. She was enthralled and after that her favorite song was "Annie." She even wanted to look like Annie and so I gave her my wig and got her tap dancing shoes so she could be Annie whenever she wanted to be. When I think back over this period they never cried when I left them in the morning, but when I left them at Greg's daycare they cried incessantly. Once when I was taking them back to Greg's home, Brit started crying and I couldn't console her. After I left her I called to see if she was okay because she was so upset, her dad told me she was fine, she wasn't crying anymore.

Catalina for New Year's: *1982*

It had been a tough year, but I had made it without injuring myself or anyone else. I received the final divorce papers from Greg's attorney. Every time I thought things were getting better there would be another letter from his attorney over the divorce or the property settlement.

I felt I was entitled to do something special for myself as a reward for making it through all the ups and downs with the divorce and custody problems. My reward was a weekend sailing trip to Catalina for New Year's Eve with the sailing club. The price included sharing the costs of gas, food and beverages. The problem with that was I was not a drinker so I was paying for the large amounts of beer the men in the club drank. It was a rule that drinking to excess was not allowed until the boat was docked. Since it was a six to eight-hour sail to Catalina the men would usually consume several beers in that amount of time. They had about ten boats sailing so I put in my name for one of the spots. I asked the branch skipper if it mattered that I was single and he said, "No, we all sit together and so there will be someone to dance with as well." Bett and I drove down with the group. She was staying with friends and I was staying with my son in his camper. The boat I was sailing on was leaving out of Long Beach Marina and my son drove me to the marina. The owners of the boat were T and J who were sailing and another lady, K. She liked to cook so I just left the cooking up to her and helped with the cleaning. We had a great trip sailing to Catalina and when all of the boats were tied up close together, we could take a short dingy ride to each one of them. I had to sleep in the galley area on the table that made out to a bed and was next to T, but we were both in separate sleeping bags and did not touch. When I sailed with the club the sleeping areas were usually decided by the owners of the boat and who their friends were. It did not bother me to share sleeping quarters and it was never a problem. Years later I met T at another club function and he didn't remember me. I reminded him that he had "slept" with me some time ago in Catalina and we all had a good laugh.

K and I ended up being the only single females in the sailing group on that trip. When we went to the ballroom I took a walk around the room and only noticed two single men alone. K had noticed them also. I went over to their table and introduced myself and told them if they would like to dance we were sitting a few tables away and would love to dance.

When we got back to our table, she said, "You know they are gay don't you?"

I told her, "Yes, I know."

Later they came over and invited us to join them at their table. We danced with them and met many people who lived on the island, since they owned a business in Catalina. When midnight came and we were dancing, they left us standing on the dance floor and passionately kissed one another. It was an experience that neither one of us would forget. The next day on New Year's Day they invited us to their condo for a brunch of black-eyed peas, cornbread, greens and champagne, which is a traditional meal for New Year's Day in order to have good luck for the following year. They took us back to our boat dock in their golf cart and we invited them to the party we were having on the boat later that evening. I am sure it gave the sailing club members a lot to talk about also, but everyone was polite and very gracious to these two men. They invited me to come back to Catalina anytime and bring my family to visit. Later when I went back with my family, Vic and her daughter, I stopped by their shop, but they were no longer there.

Job #2

I had accepted a position with more potential, but from the beginning the office had a hostile environment. I was their timekeeper and there was always a battle with the time card of one of the women. She took a great deal of sick and vacation leave and felt I should keep her apprised of what her leave balance was, when that was really her job. My boss was as supportive as he could be, but once when he was out of town, she chose that time to take her anger out on me. Her behavior was totally inappropriate. I left to go out in the hallway to cool off, and as she walked by me on her way to the lady's room she drew her hand back to hit me. I shouted to her, "Go ahead, hit me, hit me." I am sure everyone in all of the other offices heard me. Luckily, I found another position that offered more promotion potential. I was invited to the office Christmas party and a scrapbook had been made of events that took place over the year. There was a picture of Diana Ross with her hand out and the comment beside the picture was "and here's L ready to smack Barbara." She didn't like being portrayed that way and made a complaint, so that was the end of the scrapbook at the Christmas party.

The best thing about the move was that I was able to meet Sh, and we became good friends. When we answered the phone, people couldn't tell the difference between our voices. She was a very attractive African-American and said when she was growing up her family wouldn't let her talk black slang, so she had great diction. When I applied for another position with more potential she knew the manager of that office and was able to give me a good referral. I helped her with her T-shirt business one weekend in Davis at a college event. I had to get up at 5:00 a.m. and drive to Davis and she had given me the wrong directions to the motel where she was staying. I stopped at every motel up and down the highway and was eventually able to find her. By then I was angry and frustrated and blew up at her. The whole day she was cool to me and after that our friendship ended. I thought we were good friends, but I guess that was the big test, and the relationship didn't survive.

CHAPTER SEVEN

Where to Live

I thought about moving to be closer to family where I would have their mental and emotional support, but decided instead to stay in Walnut Creek so Greg could participate in raising our children. I felt I had been responsible for my two sisters at an early age, and raised my two older children mostly alone, and I did not want to raise our children on my own.

I left my first husband because of his drinking and abuse. The abuse started only six weeks after we were married. I went back to my mother's once for a few days, but knew I couldn't stay with her and by then I knew I was pregnant. I didn't want my child to grow up without their father. I wanted a two-parent family. So, I went back and hoped it wouldn't happen again. The abuse started when his former wife called and wanted to leave their daughter with us while she was going through the break-up of her latest marriage. I agreed, but only if it was going to be permanent. I knew otherwise, this was going to be a pattern with her. She eventually dropped their daughter off one night and didn't come back to see her for ten months. When she came to the door I was nine months pregnant and ready to deliver any day, and she grabbed her daughter by her hand and ran. We found out she sent her daughter to her sister's house in Missouri to live. After several months she started forging checks on our account. When we stopped mailing the checks she brought his daughter back from Missouri and dropped her off again and didn't come back for several years.

The abuse continued and by then I had a second child. I knew one of us was going to get hurt, as he had started buying and collecting guns. Someone with his drinking problem and temper should have never been able to buy a gun, but since he was an ex-marine it was something that gave him something to brag about to his co-workers. My cousin came several times late at night to pick me up when the abuse became physical. He was always there to help me when I had no one else to call. My daughter recently asked me what happened to turn her dad to being abusive and drinking. I told her I think being in the Korean War probably changed him. A person is changed mentally after they have been taught to kill another human. Some men are able to deal with the war memories, others are not.

When Bett and FJ were four and five years old I left again, and was able to find an apartment that was close to a bus route since I didn't have a car. I found a job before leaving and had taken the furniture I needed. The neighbors knew we were having problems since I had called the police on him when he was drinking and was abusive. I guess they didn't know it was so bad that I would leave.

My mother moved in with me for a short time, but ended up not staying after we had a disagreement. Her drinking had become a problem so I couldn't depend on her with the children. I was working and found a great babysitter, who was an older woman who really liked my children. I was lonely and still trying to make things work so I continued to see their dad on weekends with the kids. He was more attentive and I felt he knew that I would leave if his behavior did not change. I moved back to the house, and as soon as the last item was off the truck, he did a 360-degree change back to his old self. I made a promise that exact moment that when I moved again it would be permanent.

In the fall I decided to enroll in the local community college. I didn't discuss it, just told my husband what I was going to do. My classes were in the evening after he was home from work so he would be there with the children. After my first semester I applied for scholarships and was able to get through school with that assistance. My mother helped me as much as she could and I took a job working 10 p.m. until 6 a.m. at the Government Printing Office two nights a week to help with the gas and other expenses of school. My former husband was not going to be supportive and made things as difficult for me as he could, hoping I would drop out of school. When his shift changed at work I needed a car and he was not agreeable to helping me to buy one. My mother would have cosigned for me, but her credit was not good since she didn't have regular income due to her waitressing jobs. I went to a few car dealers, but I couldn't buy a car in Maryland without his signature. I finally was able to find a car dealer that would sell me a car, but it was not the car I wanted. It was the one they wanted to get rid of. After I was able to buy the car, when he wanted to sabotage me and didn't want me to get to school he would go out to my car and take the distributor cap off so I couldn't start the car. I finally had to have the local garage put a chain on my hood so it couldn't be opened without the key. We hadn't slept together for almost six months, he was sleeping downstairs in the bedroom he built for our company.

My Sisters Come for a Visit

My sisters called and wanted to come for a visit. Mother and I were excited to have them come since we had the extra bedroom downstairs. A few days before they arrived they called again and told me Prip was pregnant. She wasn't sure what she was going to do once she arrived, but we would solve that problem once they arrived. If they hadn't been visiting, we probably would not have been in the same bed again, and it was then I became pregnant. I knew immediately I was pregnant even without going to the doctor. My breasts were tender and the smell of coffee and bacon made me sick. My sisters and I went horseback riding, as I thought that would make me have a miscarriage, but it didn't work. I tried running up and down the stairs over and over. I went jogging, hoping that would work. After a few months they went back to California to have the baby, as my sister expected to get back with the father of the baby. He called to convince her to come back and work things out. Mother had talked to her about them getting an apartment and living together and keeping the baby if she didn't want to give it up for adoption. It was her decision and we were there for her whatever that decision was. She thought going back to California was the best for her and the baby.

After they left I read in the Sunday papers about doctors in New York who would help women who wanted to terminate their pregnancy. I started calling each one on the list and each time was referred to someone closer until I found one in Washington, DC. Before the doctor would do the procedure, I had to go to a psychologist that would verify having this child would affect my physical and mental health. I had to pay for all of these expenses from my part-time job so it meant not going back to school for the following year. I received a teaching grant from the University of Maryland for the remaining two years of my education, and agreed that I would teach for two years in Maryland to repay the grant. After the procedure was completed and I came home from the hospital my former husband started calling me baby killer. I knew then that going to school was not going to be possible and I left again for the last time. I told my step-daughter if she wanted to come with me she could, but she did not want to leave her school and friends. Several years later when she came to California to spend the summer with me, she wanted to stay because her dad was never home, he was always out drinking, but he wouldn't let her stay.

I had moved to California to be closer to my sisters. Bett and FJ were with me during the school year and the summers they were with their dad. I had been responsible for someone else since I was seven and now I was almost forty. I expected financial, physical and psychological help from Greg with our children. I told him he was not going to help someone else to raise her child and desert his own children. He was going to participate in their upbringing. The amount of child support awarded did not even cover the cost of a babysitter for both of them and I never knew when I was going to receive a check from him. I never had to beg or ask Bett and FJ's dad for a check. It was always there on time. He even paid me child support when they were with him for the summer to help with my house expenses. He only paid me twenty-five dollars a week for each of them so it wasn't a great deal of money to him, but at that time my house payment was over half of my net monthly income.

CHAPTER EIGHT

The Big Sail

I met Jm through one of the dinners I had at my house for the singles group. He lived on his forty-foot sailboat and liked to take a group of ladies out for a sail. He had a rule no men, just women. I already made up my mind that I wasn't going to get involved with him since I knew he wasn't going to be monogamous. He had been planning for some time to sail from San Francisco to Catalina. He needed people with sailing experience to sign on for the sail to help him get there. I was interested, but didn't know very much about sailing at that time. I wanted to become a skipper with the sailing club in order to take boats out on my own. I wasn't able to devote the time so far due to working full-time, taking care of the house and yard plus two small children. My children were to be with their dad for that week and I accumulated enough vacation leave to make the trip, and all it was going to cost me was my airfare back home. I was really very excited about the sail and amazingly not afraid. Bett took me to the boat at the marina and before I left I gave my will to her. She thought because I was leaving my will that I thought something might happen. I wasn't sure how good a swimmer I was, but I knew if I went overboard it might be difficult to get me out in time, because in the Bay Area the water was very cold. Another thing that would work against anyone's rescue would be the fact that we usually had on a lot of clothing, jeans, socks, shirt and sweater, shoes, along with a coat, hat and gloves. Since this was summer I usually had on my bathing suit and shorts underneath my clothes, so when the weather was nice I could easily take off a few layers.

I was to be the cook and Jm stocked the boat with all of our food and other supplies needed. His friend Bd was going, but his wife was afraid of sailing and did not want to be on the water for this length of time. Another member of the team was Ad. He was a young kid going to college and was off for the summer. We started off at about 10 a.m. on Saturday morning and sailed to the Golden Gate Bridge. The currents at the "Potato Patch" were keeping us from sailing outside the bay that night, so we turned around and moored outside of Ghirardelli Square. I fixed dinner and we enjoyed the lights from the boat, it was a beautiful sight. The next morning, we started out early for the Golden Gate in order to get out while the currents were in our favor. Once we were out it was great sailing on a beautiful sunny day. As the day progressed though the winds got stronger and increased to forty knots. Jm was afraid we were going to turn over, so he kept throwing things to the back of the boat with a line attached that would slow us down. Whatever he could put a rope on that was extra weight went over the back of the boat. We went out one-hundred miles off the coast so we wouldn't be in the shipping channel. That way we didn't have to worry about getting smashed by the bigger ships, as they wouldn't be able to stop if we were in their way. Ad was working on the Avian that was an automatic pilot system, so we wouldn't have to steer the boat all the way down. It's a good thing we had him on, because Jm was so stressed out he couldn't concentrate. He kept complaining of chest pains and we were worried he was having a heart attack. He kept saying it was just stress from getting his boat ready for the trip and feeling responsible for everyone. The winds were so strong it was impossible to do much cooking. For breakfast I usually made oatmeal with some type of canned fruit, and for lunch I made sandwiches. It was hard keeping the sandwiches on the table and several times I had to pick the ingredients up off the floor and start over again. Dinner was usually a hearty soup with whatever was available in the canned goods. When it was my turn to sleep I had to hang onto the side or else be thrown out of the bunk. I usually took the watch from 2 a.m. until 6 a.m. Since we were on automatic pilot all I had to do was watch for logs and big ships, and make sure we stayed on course. I was always tied in on both sides of the boat so I didn't have to worry about being thrown overboard while everyone slept. It wasn't easy going to bathroom, as I had to take off my many layers of clothing and still hold on with one hand to keep from being thrown about. This went on for four days until we reached Los Angeles and then the winds were one and a half knots. Jm didn't want to use the motor, he was concerned about conserving fuel. I told him we were never going to get to Catalina unless we turned on the motor. I sailed in this area with my sailing club so I knew about the winds here. As we were coming in to LA we saw a Coast Guard ship come our way, but then turn around and head back out to sea. We didn't give it much thought, but later they came after us again. I am sure they knew they would not have any trouble finding us since we were going so slow. They came up beside us again and this time over the loud speaker, told us to all come to topside and to keep our hands by our side. They knew from their radar we had been close to a hundred miles off shore. At that time, they were inspecting boats looking for illegal drugs, and they would impound them for even one marijuana cigarette. We all stood perfectly still while they boarded us and had their guns on us from the other boat. Jm took them all over the boat for their inspection. I had a roast in the pressure cooker and peach cobbler in the oven for our first decent dinner. I was worried it was going to be spoiled, but Jm saved the day and turned everything off. We passed their inspection and they left. It was then that Ad told us of the marijuana cigarette he had rolled up in his sleeping bag. It was a good thing they didn't find it, because Jm told him if the Coast Guard had taken his boat for his stupidity, he would have killed him. After that delay we were still floundering in the water with no wind and it was getting late in the day. Since we wanted to arrive at Catalina before dark Jm decided to use the motor. When we arrived on the island I told all of them I was taking a shower and changing clothes and I expected them to do the same. We all had been in the same clothes for almost five days and the odor was something awful.

I didn't have much time to spend in Catalina, as I had to get back to Long Beach and catch my plane back to the Bay Area. He had another group coming to help him bring his boat back, but that was going to be a much tougher trip as he was going against the currents.

～～～～～

Bett and the Tea Dances

I usually went to the tea dance on Friday night after work. It wasn't always easy to depend on when Greg was going to pick up the children. It was hard to make plans, but when I went I danced so much my feet ached. It was great just to watch the people and hear the wonderful music, especially when they had the harps and violins after the tea dance. When Bett started her job in the city she would join me when she got off of work. The first time she came to the dances I told her that as long as someone was not drunk or obnoxious it was not polite to turn down a request to dance. I said this after a young man just asked her to dance and she had said no. Then a man who was in his 80s came up to ask her to dance and she danced with him. That young man looked at her dance with that old man and I couldn't help but see the perplexed look on his face.

The house had been for sale for nine months and because interest rates were still high, we didn't receive any offers from buyers. Bett and I had an argument one morning as I was rushing to get Brit and Case to the babysitter and meet our van pool on time. I left my pocketbook in the house and locked the door. Bett didn't come home with me that night, as she was still hurt over comments I made. When I arrived home, I couldn't get into the house. I called our real estate agent and he was not available. Then I called another agent I worked with and asked if I could borrow her lockbox key. She was very trusting to let me borrow her lockbox key. I still had my children in the car and I drove to her office to pick up the key, drove home and unlocked the door, and then went back to return the lockbox key. When I finally got back home my neighbor next door, who was on the board of directors for the homeowner's association, had put my trash cans in my driveway and in my walkway as a reminder to put my trash cans away. When I saw this, I had no more energy left, I was drained. I wanted to put those trash cans in the middle of the street and then see what it would do to her. I remember putting the kids in bed with their clothes on and giving them just a bottle for dinner. I didn't even have the energy to take off my own clothes. I just crawled into bed fully dressed. That was one of the lowest points. I guess this was one time I let things get to me. It was usually when I was tired and not getting enough rest.

This same neighbor came to my house one time when I was at work and wanted my work number from my babysitter. She thought she could intimidate a young girl into giving her my number. Evidently the trash was not picked up, and I couldn't understand why. I realized I had not received a bill, it had probably gone to Greg and he had not forwarded it to me. I figured no problem, they will send me another bill and when I pay the bill they will pick up the trash. She was the one who threatened to call child welfare because she thought my babysitter was not taking proper care of my children. They eventually moved to another house but lost it due to her husband losing his job. It's too bad she didn't follow my example and rent out a room and take any low-paying job she could to keep her house.

One of the men from the sailing club was an attorney and he came over to discuss my taking legal action against the homeowner's association. I showed him the letters I had been receiving and explained they did not like the fact I had roommates in my home. While we were talking a neighbor came over to ask me to shut my upstairs bedroom window because my children were making too much noise with their laughing and playing. He was amazed at how petty some people were. I finally had to write a letter to the homeowner's association stating if the harassment did not stop I would start legal action. I guess their attorney advised them that I probably had a good case against them, because the harassment stopped.

<hr />

Bett and L

Bett was enjoying working, going to school in the evenings, and on the weekends when my children were with their dad, she and I would pal around together.

She was dating and going out in the evening to find "Mr. Right." She had gone out one evening and didn't come home until the morning. It was 2:00 a.m. and I started vacuuming, thinking it would take my mind off things. It was a good thing at the time I had no roommates. When she came home the following day, I asked her, "Why didn't you call me? You know I am always up." I was extremely upset that she would do this to me. I had enough on my mind without having to worry if she was dead or hurt someplace. I told her I had enough to deal with and couldn't handle any more than I was already carrying. She promised me the next time she was going to be out all night that she would call. She stayed out again and didn't call me. This time there was a big blowup. I told her that if she did it one more time she could move. I was not going to spend any more time worrying about her and if she was okay. She knew I was serious.

She met L at work. They had gone out after work on Friday night, and again she didn't come home. When she came home Saturday morning, she said she was moving in with him. He had a house on the Delta and they were going to live together and commute to work together. I didn't feel good about her moving in with him so soon after meeting, but she was an adult and made her own decisions. I had gotten used to her friendship and companionship, and would really miss her. I knew I was going to be lonely without her and couldn't help but cry when she moved. I don't think I was prepared for her to move so suddenly. I wondered if she was worried I would put her out on the street if she stayed out one more time without calling me. The only good was that at least this way I knew where she was and hoped she would be okay. Now, maybe I wouldn't have to worry about her ending up dead in a ditch some place. She was paying me some rent, so I would lose that income until I could find another roommate.

The commute was a long one from where she lived in

Discovery Bay to the Bay Area, and with trying to attend classes in the evening, her education became less of a priority. I am not sure that L encouraged or supported her plan to finish school. I think he was afraid of losing her to someone else if she got smarter and better educated, he might not appeal to her anymore. I know they had a lot of fun together, but drinking was a big part of their life.

<hr />

The Car

It was the day before my birthday and I was interviewing a prospective roommate. She was a professional female who had just moved to the area and was looking for a temporary place to live that was a clean, quiet, and safe environment. We had been talking for about twenty minutes when the doorbell rang. I went to the door and there was a man there with his tow truck. He had been instructed by the bank I was leasing the car from to pick up a check for $4,000 or the car. We leased the car while I was in real estate and I had been making the lease payments on the car and just sent in my latest payment. I had not received any notice from them that the lease was up, or that I needed to pay the residual value or give the car back. They had been in contact with Greg and he had not relayed any of the information to me. I explained to the driver, "I just sent in my payment, why are they taking the car?" It didn't make sense. The upholstery was not in good shape because I always had food or drink for the kids whenever we went out of the house. The tow truck driver told me I needed to take my belongings out of the car, as he was going to take the car on orders from the lender. I took out my belongings and he drove off with the car. I was glad it was late at night and my neighbors would not know what was going on. It was very embarrassing and demoralizing to have this happen to me. When I went back to talk with the prospective roommate I knew she was embarrassed for me. Here I was living in this five-bedroom house in Walnut Creek and seemed to have my life together and a lot going for me, and my car was being repossessed. After she left I called Greg to find out why he didn't let me know what was going on with the car. This was very mean-spirited of him, and not very honorable. He told me he wanted us to talk the way we once were able. We never had a problem communicating until the break-up. I told him he couldn't have two wives. That night I called my dad, my mother and my sister to tell them what had happened. I was very upset, and I couldn't stop crying. I didn't ask for the money from anyone and especially not my parents, as their only income was from Social Security. I had never asked for money from family or friends and couldn't do so now. The next day I didn't go to work, but called several banks to see if I could get a loan. The banks all had the same response, "No, your expenses are too high for your income." Even the IRS wanted to know how I could make it on my income, so I was audited several times to prove my income and deductions. I called Bett and told her what happened and she said they would help me by giving me a ride into the city. They went out of their way in order to give me a ride and it made their commute even longer. I didn't know how I was going to be able to pick up my children on my weekends, go grocery shopping, or to make the many other errands I would have to take care of my house.

～～～～～

Back to Real Estate

I knew I wasn't going to be able to make ends meet on my salary and any child support I received from Greg. I had been working in a real estate office down the street on evenings and weekends when I didn't have my children. I started working on expired listings in the area. Since I was working full-time in the city, my partner Bn would take messages and talk with my clients for me when I was not available. Without a car I would have to give up real estate. There was no way I could meet with buyers regarding listing their property, hold open houses, or show property without my car. I lost two nights of sleep and a day of work crying due to my car being repossessed. When I called Bn I told him I had something to tell him and it was confidential. I didn't want him sharing my story with anyone else. I had resigned myself to the fact that I wouldn't have a car. I would take the bus to the BART station, and as for groceries I would walk to the grocery store which was about a mile down the road, and only buy what I could carry. I had determined that my car, insurance costs and maintenance were costing me almost $300 per month, and this was money I could use elsewhere. As for my children, Greg would have to do the driving to bring them to me. Bn called me back and asked my permission to tell our boss about the car. I told him, "Okay, but no one else." Bn called me back and said that our boss had a car he had co-signed for another real estate agent who defaulted on the loan, and he had to repossess the car. I could have the use of the car and all I had to do was to take over the payments. I couldn't believe it, I lost two nights of sleep and a day of work and all I had to do was tell one person and the solution to my problem was presented. The car hadn't been taken good care of, and didn't have air conditioning, but it was an answer to my prayers. I don't know how I could have so little faith that things would work out, but to me this was a real test.

Bn was a great help to me while we worked together. He also was going through a divorce and we compared our experiences with former spouses and child raising challenges. At Christmas time he had a Santa Claus costume and was making stops at various friends in the neighborhood. I asked him if he had time to come and visit my house, as my family and children were all there. He agreed and I left a Christmas gift outside the door for Brit and Case so when he came in the door he gave them their gift. Case was too young to appreciate his visit. He was afraid of this stranger with a beard and a red suit, but Brit was so happy and kept hugging his legs. It was a great time for my sisters also, for all of us to be together. I am sure this was a difficult Christmas for Prip since this was the first Christmas after the death of her son. She couldn't get enough time holding both of my children.

CHAPTER NINE

Jason: *January 1983*

I met Jason at the tea dance, but the first time he asked me to dance I wasn't attracted to him. His mustache wasn't attractive to me, as he was attempting to have it curl on the ends like a handlebar. After the dance, he took me to dinner at my favorite restaurant, and then he drove me to BART for the train home. I called him the next day and invited him to my house for a barbeque. I knew if I didn't see him that weekend I would not be available for two more weekends since it would be my time to have my children. When he arrived for dinner, he was wearing a plaid shirt and Levi's which suited him better. He also trimmed his mustache which greatly improved his appearance and I knew immediately there was an attraction. After dinner we went to the restaurant at the golf course where they had music and dancing. I told him when I called with the invitation that I had an extra bedroom if he wanted to spend the night. He stayed for the weekend, but not in the extra bedroom, and after that we were together most weekends. It was difficult parting after such a great weekend.

BARBARA SHAW

The next weekend I stopped by his shop when I picked up my children, and we went out for pizza with his two daughters. Since I was a package deal I wanted him to meet them as soon as possible. He saw I had a different car from the previous weekend and asked me why I had a different car. I said it was a long story, but I would tell him later when we were alone. After I told him what happened he seemed to be suspicious about why someone I worked for would be loaning me a car. I explained that I was doing him a favor by taking the car off his hands, since he didn't have to make car payments any longer, and it certainly was a lifesaver for me.

When I had my children, he would come over on Friday or Saturday and we would go to the park or swim at the community pool. On Monday morning he would drive me to work and take Case and Brit to their daycare since it was on his way home. On those Mondays when I got out of the car Case would cry and scream, as he didn't want me to leave. It was tough leaving them, and I know this was difficult for him. I don't know why Jason volunteered to do this for me. I felt their life shouldn't be like this. I didn't plan on having two more children, to work full-time and leave them at a daycare center before the crack of dawn. Our first time camping I drove to the city to meet him. I was in such a hurry I got into the express lane, as I usually did when I commuted during the week. I went past the toll taker, and needless to say I was stopped by a police officer on a motorcycle. The ticket cost me sixty dollars. One of the attorneys I worked with said I could probably fight it if I wanted to, but I knew I was wrong. Why would I want to lie and make a fool of myself in front of a judge in court?

I parked my car near where I worked and we drove to Santa Rosa to pick up his camper, which was very clean and comfortable. He had taken good care of it, so it was always great to go camping. The next day we took off for the coast and spent the night in the camper, cooking dinner, listening to music and playing cards, for a wonderful evening. We returned the camper to his brother's and spent the night there leaving for work the next morning very early.

After that, our first long trip was to Tijuana. I had a long weekend from work so we drove to Fresno and stayed with my sister and her husband. He liked both of them and enjoyed watching them banter back and forth, each one trying to have the last word. My sister's husband had previously told me I should consider myself lucky Greg left me when I was under forty, since I was still young and attractive enough to be able to find another mate or companion. I guess he assumed I would be able to meet someone again and remarry.

When we arrived in Tijuana it was great just to lie out by the pool in the sun, just read and lounge. Jason had his favorite places to go to dinner. He was always looking for a place with a view so we could watch the sun go down. Sometimes we drove for miles looking for a restaurant with a view. Our trip was wonderful, almost like a honeymoon. On Sunday before we left we went to a swap meet and I bought Case a two-wheel bike for ten dollars. It was so cute and just his size to learn how to ride a two-wheeler. I also bought them both some used cowboy boots. Since their feet grew so fast I got them a little bigger so they would last longer. I told Jason now they could have their "poor me stories about the bike and the cowboy boots my mom bought in Tijuana."

~~~~~~~~~~

Easter

The first Easter we were together, Jason came over on Saturday and his brother came also to meet my roommate, Kat. He had broken up with his girlfriend and was looking for a new companion and a new relationship. I had a full house with Brit, Case, my sister, my son FJ, my future daughter-in-law, and Bett came with L. We had a barbeque on Saturday and went to church on Sunday. Jason's brother spent the night on the couch and my sister was in a spare bedroom. Jason's cousin and his wife stopped by to say hello on Saturday, and added to the party-like atmosphere. We talked, we joked and we laughed a lot that weekend, but after church Jason left to have Easter dinner with his mother and father. I was disappointed because I thought this was going to be our day together. I didn't realize this was going to be a pattern, and that this would be a problem for us for the next seven years we were together. We took pictures and I remember how happy and blessed I felt that day. It was one of the happiest days I had since Christmas.

~~~~~~~~~~

Case to the Hospital

One weekend when Case and Brit were with me and I was bathing them, Case cried every time I touched his arm. I could see his arm was swollen and I knew he needed to be looked at by a doctor. When I was in the emergency room with him the doctor attending him said his arm had been pulled out of its socket. He had to twist the arm back into place. It was painful to watch the doctors working on him and to hear him crying. When we went home I called Greg and said someone had been picking him up by his arm. I told him Case was a big boy and he should not be pulled by his arm. I told him to give the daycare center instructions on this.

The director of the daycare center called me to talk about Case's aggressive behavior. I told her he was only repeating the behavior he learned at their daycare center. I told her of his arm being jerked out of its socket and the visit to the emergency room, and said it probably happened at the daycare center. Previously when I picked them up from the daycare center I could see there were several unhappy children and fighting amongst them. I felt he was only sticking up for himself. It wasn't a happy time for them to be dropped off at the daycare center. The crying was hard to handle. When I dropped them off at the daycare in Walnut Creek they were never as emotional about me leaving them. They never cried.

When they were with me in the summer we spent most evenings and weekends at the pool. I would pack veggies to snack on until dinner, and we went to the pool to cool down. Case started swimming on his own when he was still in diapers. I would let him go around the outside of the pool and could see him hanging on to the concrete when he needed a rest. I saw other fathers trying to get their sons do the same thing. They didn't realize they couldn't force their children to not be afraid of the water. What Case did came naturally to him. When someone asked him how he breathed under water, he told them, "I breathe through my ears." I called him my "little otter." One of our pastors was a swim coach and I asked him if Case could join his class. I told him he could be an Olympic champion. He saw how positive I was about his ability and he agreed to take him into his class, but Case did not want to wear a Speedo swimsuit. No chance to be an Olympic champion, and I was so sure he could be.

FJ, My Grandson

When my grandson was born my son decided one morning out of the blue they were going to go to church as a family.

On their way out of the church the minister asked, "Has the baby been baptized?" He said, "No."

The minister said, "Well, we'll have to get him baptized." Then he asked, "Are mom and dad married?"

He again said, "No."

Then the minister said, "Well, we'll have to take care of that also. The man upstairs is not happy about that."

I drove to Lancaster for the baptism, and Bett and L also came. It was a nice ceremony for the baby. Then a couple of weeks later the wedding was planned. Jason joined Brit and Case and I for the trip down. Brit was to be a flower girl and was going to wear her Easter outfit for the ceremony.

I asked Bett if she and L would pick up Brit, and Jason and I would take Case with us just to make the trip easier.

When I picked them both up and they saw they were going in separate cars it made me realize how dependent they were on each other. It didn't matter that their mom and dad weren't together, what mattered was that they were not going to be separated. Case especially depended on Brit, she was always there to take care of him when Greg or I were not there. At one time he wanted to split the children up, for me to take one of them and him to take one, just like the furniture.

I told him, "No, they will stay together."

The wedding was a simple affair. The bride bought a wedding dress off the rack and had fancy floral arrangements and flowers. I was going to make appetizers for the reception.

My son asked me, "Can you make our wedding cake?"

He remembered I made my own cake when Greg and I got married.

I told him, "It takes days to put together a wedding cake, and I cannot do it in such short amount of time."

When I made my own wedding cake I started days ahead, made six cakes and put them in the freezer to assemble the day before the wedding. They decided to buy a cake from the local bakery, had a keg of beer and champagne, and ordered a mile-long board sandwich, which worked out great. We all sat outside on the grass, some in lawn chairs and blankets while they opened presents. Mother and dad had driven down as well. We checked into a motel and mother stayed with the bride's parents and they continued partying. I was not into drinking that much, especially when I had to take care of Brit and Case. Mother ended up not being able to find her way back to the motel and had to spend the night with the party people. When I met the family of the bride-to-be, I listened to their stories and I realized what a rough life they all had. My son had been laid off his job and was on unemployment for a year. He was waiting for a training program with a large corporation, but if he took a job he wouldn't be eligible for the training. He also could not turn down any job that was offered to him. Luckily, he found temporary employment to hold him over until he received an offer for the program. I told him once that our family doesn't take welfare and stay on unemployment for an extended time. He finally was called to work, but I think his wife missed his company when he went back to work full-time. My son told her she could go to work if she wanted, or return to school for further education. When she left the marriage and moved out of state my son went to an attorney for custody of his son. We were worried about him being so far away from home if something should happen to his mother. She finally came back, but it was too late for the marriage. When my son decided to get the divorce, he called me and it was so sad to hear him, he was crushed. I guess the only thing I could say was "I am so sorry." I remembered when they stayed with us for Christmas and how happy their son was. She did not realize how this was going to affect her son and the pain it would cause him. He missed his mother. He stayed with his other grandmother when my son was working overtime. He had a daily work schedule of six days a week, with ten hours a day. She helped him out a great deal and made up for the time he was not with his mother. I don't think he realized how hard it is to be a single parent because he had so much help from the other grandmother.

<p style="text-align:center">~~~~~~</p>

Catalina

I planned on going to Catalina on the 4th of July with Vi and her daughter. Bett, L, FJ, and his wife also joined us. FJ and Bett's dad was visiting them for the summer, and wanted to know if he could attend also with his girlfriend.

I said, "Sure."

I didn't expect their dad to travel all that distance and not spend time with them. He avoided any contact while I was married to Greg. He came to California for Bett and FJ's graduation but chose not to come to the house afterward for a small gathering to celebrate the event. I am sure his spouse at that time did not feel comfortable meeting and socializing, but his present girlfriend was not intimidated at all by our previous relationship. The weekend turned out to be a great deal of fun for all of us. The only problem was when their dad was drinking. When he went into his tent to sleep, which was usually early, he expected everyone around him to go to sleep also. Since this was 4th of July weekend this was not going to happen. He got quite loud and I was not sure if the campground would renew us for another night. They only confirmed day-by-day in case they had to ask someone to leave. I bought a wagon for the kids so I could take them on walks on the bike path while they were with me. The wagon really came in handy carrying all our gear from the dock of the ferry to the camp ground, buying groceries, and getting to the beach.

I took Brit and Case to the ferry to meet Vi and her daughter. There was a park close by and Brit was on the swing, and I told her to stay right there. I was going just a few feet away to check on the ferry schedule. When I came back to the swings she was gone. I was frantic. I went up to an officer and told him I had just stepped away and my daughter was gone.

He said, "Don't worry, no one will be able to get off Catalina with her."

In the meantime, I went searching and looking in cars and vans that were parked close by. Then I found her playing just a few feet from where I left her. She found another play area where there were more children. After that I didn't trust her to stay in the same spot, and took her with me to check on the ferry. Vi and I are somewhat alike in our spending habits. We try to live within our incomes and not live on our charge cards. She and I and would have breakfast in the campground with our children, and fix sandwiches to take with us to the beach. For dinner we would look for an economical place to eat dinner. Everyone else ate most of their meals at the restaurants with their dad paying for most of the meals. Bett had gone shopping at one of the local shops and bought a stylish T-shirt with holes cut out that was in vogue at the time. I could hear my son and his wife in their tent next to me, as she wanted to buy a similar T-shirt.

He told her, "We don't have thirty dollars for a T-shirt. I'll make you a T-shirt like that with holes in it for free."

She never knew what it was like to be independent

and have her own money since she got pregnant at such a young age and never supported herself. On the 4th of July we were all invited to eat together at a local restaurant at their dad's treat. It was an evening with lots of laughter. FJ and Bett both have a great sense of humor and the banter that goes on is always amusing to me.

When I lived in Fresno their dad came to visit for several weeks. I let him use the car I was selling since I had already bought a new, used one. I also let him stay at my house and I went to my sister's. I knew it was going to be an expensive trip for him, so I tried to help him have a normal relationship with FJ and Bett when he was visiting. He called me when I first moved to Fresno, as he wanted to move there, and asked if he could stay with me until he "got on his feet." I didn't think that was a good idea. I told him if he was coming to California to get back with me it was not going to happen. I had gone back with him too many times, trying to make our marriage work. When I was buying my house in Fresno I asked him to give me my property settlement out of the house and he refused. I needed the extra funds when the bank turned me down because I didn't have any savings. I received word while I was at work that the bank turned me down for my loan. I was at my desk looking at the ads for apartments when someone came to my desk and commented about my concentration. They didn't know I was crying and had my head down. I left the office upset and to look for an apartment.

FJ and Bett kept saying, "Why aren't we moving into our new house?"

It was hard for them to understand. I decided to go

to the bank and FHA and see what I needed to do to be able to convince them I was not someone who would walk away from my responsibility and the mortgage payment. They questioned how, as a single parent, was I going to put in a lawn, and how was I going to be able to make repairs. Today they would not be able to ask questions like that. I finally was able to jump through the hoops and obtain the extra documentation they required. I think someone from the office I worked for called FHA on my behalf.

CHAPTER TEN

Dk #1

Dk was referred to rent a room in my house by someone in the singles group. He had been through several divorces and hadn't been able to make any of his marriages work. When he moved in he thought I would be his pal and companion. He invited me to have a drink in the evening and unwind with him. The second time he wanted me to join him I told him we were just room-mates and I did not feel comfortable sharing personal information about my divorce with him. I wanted to keep my life private and didn't feel like listening to his problems after my long day at work and commuting. He seemed to drink a great deal, in fact when he had a glass of wine; it was usually a large water glass of eight-plus ounces and several of them at that. One night I heard some loud noises coming from his room. I knocked on his door and asked if he was okay.

He answered, "Okay."

I could tell he was drunk. He continued to bang around in his room, but I did not want to open his door.

That had always been my rule, not to go into anyone's room without their invitation or permission unless it was an emergency. The next day when I came home he had left a note that he was having the dresser repaired that he broke and would be moving out. He couldn't stand to face me after this episode and decided to move out while I was at work. Later, his mother called to see how he was and I told her, "He moved out."

She said, "Oh, it didn't work out?"

I told her "No, he had been drinking and just moved out after having my dresser repaired."

She said, "I thought he was over that."

Later I read in the newspaper he committed suicide by jumping off one of the bridges in the area. His drinking caused him a great many problems and unhappiness, and finally caused him to take his life.

Ri the Musician

When Ri answered my ad, he presented himself as someone normal, and someone I could count on to pay his rent. When people asked me what was I looking for in a roommate I told them, "Someone who acts normal."

His goal was to make it in show business. He rearranged my living room with my furniture so his furniture would fit into the family room. He put a storage shed in my back yard for the items he couldn't get into the house and garage. He brought a complete houseful of furniture and goods from Colorado. When I came home it was quite a change. It was crowded, but looked okay, so I didn't mind. As long as my roommates didn't have junky furniture I didn't mind their furniture mixed in with mine. He also had a keyboard, a banjo and several guitars. We had a few joint dinners with different ladies he was dating. I thought this was the way I wanted it to work out. Roommates that would make up for the life and family that I was missing. He was quite personable, had been in real estate, had his own business at one time and now wanted to sing in clubs in the area. He had been dating someone in the area, but I guess she wanted to get married and he didn't. One morning one of my roommates asked if I heard them the night before. His room was next to them and they were discussing getting married.

He kept saying, "I don't want to get married. I've already done that."

His girlfriend was pushing to get married. My room was on the opposite side of the house, and I hadn't heard a thing. I knew he had been seeing other women though and probably wanted to continue to play the field. Christmas was coming, and he and his girlfriend were going away for a few days. She was out in the car waiting for him, and I told him before he left that he might want to put his guitars away since the kids were here and going to be with me for the holidays.

I was cleaning and he came into the kitchen and said, "Keep your kids away from my guitars."

I lost it when he said that. I told him, "I gave you fair warning about leaving your guitars out in the middle of the family room."

He left his pick in one of the guitars and as soon as the guitar was touched the pick fell on the floor. We went back and forth yelling and finally he left. He moved out while I was at work, without giving me notice. He left owing me money for rent, phone calls, and his share of the utilities. I traced him by his telephone calls to his father's in Sacramento. I decided I probably wouldn't be able to get the money owed me so I let it go. Sometime later an agent from the IRS came looking for him so I was able to let them know where his father was, and that he would probably know where to reach Ri. I felt I had given him payback for the money he owed me.

<hr>

Dg, Another Single Parent

Dg was a single parent who had his eighteen-month-old son every other weekend. He was a quiet, nice looking young man in his 30s. He had a girlfriend, but had stopped seeing her. She didn't want to give up and still persisted in pursuing him. At times she came to the house and waited outside for him to come in from work.

She tried to get me to let her into his room, saying, "I'm sure he wouldn't want me waiting outside."

I told her, "I can't let you into his room unless I have permission from him."

I shared my phone with roommates at that time, and she called him at all times of the night. He made it known to her that he definitely was not interested in a relationship with her. Since I was an early riser due to my work schedule I usually disconnected the phone in my room when I went to bed, and let the calls go to the answering machine. There were usually several messages from her.

She just didn't want to give up. On weekends when he had his son he said he could tell his son sensed when it was Sunday evening and time to go back to his mother, the transition time. After he said that I realized Brit and Case would go through the same thing when they had to leave and go back to their dad. After he moved he continued to get mail from the Church of Scientology. I wasn't sure what his philosophy about religion was, as we never talked very much. I was usually up very early commuting to work and went to bed early. Several weekends when we both had our children we would meet in the kitchen or the family room. I know he kept his son in his room most of the time because of all the things he would get into.

<hr />

Kat

Kat had just returned from the Peace Corps in South America and had a child from a relationship there. She was renting two rooms, one for her daughter and one for herself. I thought it would be nice to have another female in the house with a child for a family atmosphere for Brit and Case and not have people who just wanted to use my house to party. Jason's brother came over one weekend to meet Kat and we were going to play cards and have a barbeque. I guess there wasn't any chemistry between them. One thing against her was the fact she had a child and he didn't want children. He knew that before he came, but I guess he didn't have anything better to do and was curious about where I lived. In addition, the commute to Walnut Creek from Santa Rosa was going to be too long. She seemed to have eyes for Jason though, and kept putting her hand on his shoulder, and making eye contact with him constantly.

Bett thought she was making a play for her boyfriend at the same time. She was a big flirt, I finally decided. Her daughter seemed to have a problem with inappropriate touching. She was the same age as Brit, but once when we were in the car she kept trying to put her hands on Brit's private parts, so I had to keep watching her when they played together. She didn't stay very long though. She finally moved where she had a better job offer, and was able to rent a house for what her two rooms cost in Walnut Creek.

~~~~~~~~~~~~

KP

KP was from Thailand. I was impressed when he came to the interview and took his shoes off. He smoked, but it was only to be in his room. I didn't think it would bother me if he smoked only in his room. This was a rule that I later changed, as no matter where a person smoked in the house, it smelled all over the house. He was a short order cook for a restaurant and did a lot of cooking for himself when he was home. He seemed to be quiet and I never heard much from him. It wasn't until after I decided to rent the house and move when I picked up the phone one evening to make a call and KP was on the other line. He was calling the police to report someone took his orange juice. I told the police I would handle things. I realized he really was not all together if he called the police for such a trivial matter.

I wanted a break from the roommate situation and decided to rent the entire house to a couple. When I had to show his room, I realized what a pack rat he was. He kept every newspaper he ever received from Thailand. I told him this was a fire hazard and he had to get rid of them. I had to be careful how I approached him, as I didn't want him to come after me with the meat cleaver when preparing his meals. I started making sure my room door was locked at night when I was having problems with him or the other males in the house, but most of the time I was not afraid of my roommates. I was not a sound sleeper since I was usually getting up when I heard my children cry or move around.

Mn

Mn was a law student. He seemed to be a nice, quiet young man. I had a rule of no overnight guests of the opposite sex except for long-term relationships. He said he had a girlfriend in San Jose and she wouldn't be over that often, because he had to study. One night he went out to party, and brought someone home. I could hear him getting her out of the house before I got up. She called him several times, thinking this was going to be a relationship and not just a one-night stand.

We had a disagreement over the phone and utility bills. I always put all the bills out on the counter for all to look at and divided the amount by how many days they had been renting. If anything, I always thought I was more than fair and it was usually in their favor. He kept on arguing and wouldn't let it go. He wanted to argue and I finally said that was the way it was going to be, issue closed. His response was, "Who made you queen bee?"

I said, "I am captain of this ship and I will make the final decision."

When he moved he didn't leave me a forwarding address, but called me and wanted a refund on his rent. I told him I would have sent him a final statement, but he did not leave me his address. I guess he wanted to try out his legal education on me. It usually took me a couple of weeks for all of the bills to come in and to make sure all the telephone charges were in before I could give back any refunds.

CHAPTER ELEVEN

Lake Sequoia

Vi called to see if we were interested in going to Lake Sequoia for camping during the summer. It had been a few years since we had been back. The last time was when Brit was eighteen months old. Lynn, Prip, her husband, Ro and Nk, along with Bett, went that time. We rented one of the cabins by the lake. We had a wonderful day lying by the lake with the children playing in the playpen. All went well until it turned dark and the frogs started making their usual noise. At night the sound was magnified because of the quietness. We took Brit to bed with us, but as soon as we turned the lights out she started screaming. She was frightened by the dark and the sound of the frogs. I took her outside and we stayed in the car all night, sleeping in snatches as much as I could. By morning I was exhausted but was ready to stay another night since I had been able to nap during the day by the lake. Everyone was so exhausted from losing sleep, they all wanted to go home early. That was the last time we went for several years.

We started camping at Lake Sequoia in 1973 when we

found the camp by accident. We had been looking for a family place and saw the small sign on the side of the road when we were going to Sequoia National Park, and decided to see what facilities they had. After seeing they had tent sites for camping, which we preferred, as well as canoes, rowboats, sailboats, and paddle boats. At night we had our own camp fire, crafts, artwork, and hiking programs, and it was very affordable. I was looking for a place for when FJ and Bett returned home after visiting with their dad for the summer. This was a way for them to readjust and get back into the mode of living with mom again. Vi usually brought her daughter camping, and Bett and FJ brought their friends from the neighborhood—Yv and J.

On one trip, J put his tennis shoes too close to the fire to dry out and the soles melted. Since he didn't have any extra shoes and he had small feet Vi loaned him her wedge sandals until we could find him a replacement in the lost and found the next morning. It was a funny picture, him walking around in her sandals. We had many great memories from our camping trips. This was a new generation to take camping. Brit and Case loved it, and so did their mom. They could participate in whatever program they wanted and Vi and I could sit on the beach in our lawn chairs and read, talk, and swim. FJ and my grandson joined us and this began our yearly trip to Lake Sequoia. We reconnected with the same families each year and watched how all the children grew and what directions in life they took. This was my one way of keeping our family together and connected by our experiences in the beautiful campground. Later, when my back could not take sleeping on the ground any longer we reserved a cabin and the kids were so excited the first night it was hard for them to sleep. Case's friend M always went with us and they usually spent their time fishing and asking the more experienced fishermen where the best place to fish was. The older fishermen usually got up at 4:00 a.m. and had their quota of fish by 5:30 a.m. They were not interested in getting up that early for fishing. Usually they were too impatient and were constantly moving their fishing poles to another spot. I think it was several years before one of them finally caught a fish. No matter how much stress there was in my life during the year I always knew we would have Lake Sequoia to look forward to.

~~~~~~~

Bett's Call for Help

Bett had been with L for over a year and several times Brit, Case, Jason, and I went to their place for a barbeque. It was a large house on the water with a deck. We had a good time and I could see how she would like living there. However, there was trouble in paradise. I didn't know how bad it was and to what extreme until one evening when I just picked up Brit and Case from across the bay, and like always on Friday evening the traffic was maddening. I was watching the news on television when the phone rang.

I picked up the phone and a voice I didn't recognize said, "Mom."

The voice I heard was not from someone I knew and almost hung up. Then I realized it was Bett. She had been crying and her voice was unrecognizable. She and L had been out to dinner and he hit her in the face while they were in the restaurant. She ran across the street to a beauty parlor and called me. He was outside trying to get in to talk to her, but some African-American men were there, and they weren't going to let him approach her while she was there. I put Brit and Case in the car and we went to pick her up. She came out to the car and her face was a mess where he hit her. She was crying hysterically. L came running up to the car to talk to her. The men again came after him, and he took off running. We asked them not to hurt him just to leave him alone. Lucky for him they didn't catch him. I am sure they could have caught him if they wanted to, they were just playing "cat and mouse" with him. We arrived home and L was right behind us. He came to the door, but I didn't open it, telling him to leave, or I was going to call the police.

He kept knocking at the door and I said, "The police are coming, they are on the way, you better leave before they get here."

He went down the street to a pay phone and kept calling. We had to turn the phone off to get any peace, but she gave in. She couldn't say no to him, and finally talked to him. She also called the Women's Crisis Center and talked to them about her situation. She said the Crisis Center told her they didn't think he would harm her if she went back. I think she might have misinterpreted their advice, since she did not want to give up on the relationship. So, the next morning she went back. He promised he was going to stop drinking and go to therapy. After that when they came over for dinner and we had wine we didn't offer him any, which must have been hard on him. My sisters and I stopped serving drinks at the holidays because of our parents' drinking problem and we usually didn't offer them alcoholic beverages at special occasions so this seemed normal to us. Thinking back, it was probably not a thing I would do now, to drink in front of an alcoholic. Their relationship didn't last after that episode. He reverted to his old behavior with the physical abuse. After that episode Brit did not want to go his house after what he did to Bett. I told her if Bett forgave him then God would want us to forgive him also, but she never felt the same about him after that. Later Bett called me again to help her pack and move her things. She took off work early while he was at work and wanted to have all of her belongings out before he came home. I had rented out my house and was renting a room from my friend Ke from the singles group. I was worn out living with roommates, running the ads, interviewing and selecting roommates took so much energy. There was always a lot of turnover. I felt most single people were in a transition period and my house was a respite for them until they could make a decision about their life and where to go next. She stayed the night at Ke's house after we moved all of her things. There wasn't room at Ke's house, but the neighbor next door, who was a policeman in the city, had a room she could rent. He was nice looking and I thought something might develop between them, and he was a total gentleman. He knew she was vulnerable at that time and might be getting into a relationship for the wrong reasons. L continued to call her and they met a couple

BARBARA SHAW

of times for dinner. I was concerned that she was going to get lonely or bored and move back with him, but she didn't. Luckily, they worked in separate locations so they wouldn't often run into one another, and she avoided his local hangouts. I think he was able to find someone else quickly to fill the void she left, otherwise he would have continued to harass her. We saw him in downtown Walnut Creek with a female, which explained why he left her alone.

~~~~~~~~~~~~~~

Ke, My Friend

Ke and I met at a potluck I had at my house for the singles group. It was a great mix of single people for dinner, and we enjoyed it so much we tried to make the dinners an ongoing event. It made the dinner hour so much more enjoyable to have adult conversation and companionship. It worked so well the first Thanksgiving I was alone. Bett had to work the Friday after Thanksgiving, and would be alone if we went to Fresno. A few days before Thanksgiving I only had six men RSVP for the dinner, and no women. I assumed that most single women had families or friends to have dinner with, but the men did not. Ke also decided to have a singles group at her house for Thanksgiving. She said she had seven men signed up for dinner at her house, and no women. My son FJ was driving from Southern California for the holiday, since I decided to stay in Walnut Creek in order for us all to be together. Brit and Case would be with me since it was my turn to have Thanksgiving with them.

After talking to Ke we decided to combine our groups and she volunteered to have the dinner at her house. She would furnish the turkey and was asking everyone to bring an appetizer, vegetable or wine. Her friend Ra was going to make the pies since that was his specialty. When we arrived at Ke's house, there were thirteen men.

My son FJ was not happy about the arrangement and said, "Why are you having dinner with these people? You have a family."

He didn't see the humor in the situation. The choice was to have dinner with the singles group at my house or Ke's, or have dinner by ourselves. I preferred to have dinner with the group to keep the conversation interesting.

Ke set up two tables with china, cloth napkins and real silverware which was unusual for the singles group. We were accustomed to having paper plates, paper napkins, and plastic utensils with the singles group. One table was in the dining room and one in the kitchen/family room. I stayed in the kitchen since Case was one year old and Brit was three at the time, and I knew they would probably make a mess. While we were eating, I had Case on my lap and he was enjoying himself eating out my plate with his hands, as he still hadn't mastered a fork or spoon yet. I didn't think it was such a big deal since I could wash my clothes later. It didn't bother me.

Later, one of the men from the sailing club that I had invited called me from the dining room and said, "Could you get your kids from under the table, we're trying to talk."

Case finished eating and was under the table, laying on the floor, drinking his bottle and kicking the table leg with his foot, which was disturbing to them. Ke's friend didn't want to give Brit and Case any pie for desert. He said they didn't finish the food on their plate. I thought it was amusing the way the men were acting. They forgot what it was like to be a child. I wondered what kind of fathers they were with their own children if this was a big issue. It was Thanksgiving, the usual dinner rules didn't apply then. I enjoyed myself in spite of everything, as it was nice just to enjoy adult conversation and companionship. I had been feeling very lonely and depressed, but this day was the funniest I had in several months. Both Ke and I laughed until we cried. I am not sure that my son FJ enjoyed himself. He preferred being just with family, and did not have the need for friendship and companionship that I needed. Bett had gone out after work on Wednesday with friends, and she was not in the best mood to take a family picture. I bought sailor outfits for Brit and Case and wanted us all to take a picture for a Christmas card. The picture wasn't the best as neither FJ or Bett wanted to dress for the occasion, so I ended up not sending out a family Christmas photo.

Ke started renting out rooms after she saw how I had been able to stay in my house with the help of roommates. Since I rented my house to simplify my life, and I hadn't decided where to live, she suggested I move in with her until I knew where I wanted to go. I put my furniture in storage and moved in with her and her daughter. I planned on staying until I found something that was acceptable. In the evening when I came home from work and planned on cooking my dinner the counters were not clean and the dishes were dirty in the dishwasher or in the sink. The cats had free run of the house and would be up on the counters looking for food or water and there was cat hair all over everything. The dog was forever going into the bedrooms and bringing out our dirty laundry to the living and family room area, and he especially liked our underwear.

I started looking at apartments in the city so I would be closer to Brit and Case and would be able to see them during the week when they weren't with me. It was interesting to see what was available and the price of apartments. I found a new one-bedroom apartment that was renting for $550 per month. Everything was brand new and clean, clean, clean. I was going to go back to Oklahoma to see my sister for Christmas, but decided to move on Christmas Eve instead. I said that was my Christmas present to myself, my new apartment. Ke was very easy to live with, as she was always flexible and nothing ever bothered her. It was a great place to stay for a short time and think about where I wanted to be. I was able to have Brit and Case with me while I was at her house, but sharing my bed was not easy for the three of us. She had a swimming pool that she kept covered when not in use, so I was never able to relax when they were there. They would walk around the pool and throw their toys in and then try to retrieve them. It was a game for them, but it scared me to leave them even for a minute.

When Brit was a year old she fell into our spa in Southern California and I found her floating face down. I had gone to show property early in the morning and FJ was to put the trash cans out by the curb. When I came home I heard the trash truck going up the street. He had not put the trash cans out, so we ran up the street chasing them with our cans. I had a terrible thought about Brit and the spa, so I ran back to the house and found her floating face down. I jumped in with clothes and shoes on and picked her up, she sputtered and spit water out of her mouth, but was okay. We were lucky that time. I did not ever want that experience to be repeated.

Property Settlement

Greg and I had partners on two homes in Southern California. Our partner and his wife were living in our home and wanted to buy Greg out, but he would not negotiate with them. He ended up going to a real estate agent I formerly worked with and she charged a commission to handle the sale. Needless to say, this made our partners angry that he would pay a commission, but would not work with them on the price. They moved into the house and we were to be two-thirds owners until mortgage rates went down and then they would refinance and buy us out. The other house we had was rented by a friend of mine. I wanted to move back to this house and go back to my previous job. When I made this offer to Greg he responded, "You are going to have to pay top price to get into that house."

Our tenant was not willing to move out.

She said, "I have been through a lot, and since you and Greg have plenty of money, you can find something else."

Her boyfriend was going to buy the house for her, but he didn't want to close escrow until his divorce was final.

He didn't want that house to complicate his divorce settlement. I finally decided I guess God doesn't want me to move back to LA. He must want me here in Walnut Creek.

The house was due to close escrow in a few days when our other partner called me and said, "Will you call and talk to her? I can't talk to her."

I told him, "I can't call now, but will call later when I am at home."

A few minutes later she made the mistake of calling me at work and I told her, "We agreed on your price and your terms, now either close escrow on time or get out of the house, and don't ever call me again."

The other partner finally had to buy me out and close escrow with her. Years later I decided to go by and say hello.

She made the comment, "You tried to get me out of this house, and M tried to get me out of this house into a bigger house, but I am never leaving this house."

I received a card occasionally, but I really didn't want to pursue a friendship with her after what had happened on the house purchase. When Greg and I were together she called me numerous times unloading on the many things she was going through, talking for hours. He constantly told me to hang up on her. I told him I couldn't, she needed someone to talk to, she was having a difficult time. Some years later I ran into her again at the shopping center. I almost didn't recognize her, but she recognized me. Her husband died and she was having a difficult time dealing with the loss.

She told me, "It was wrong what we did to you when you wanted to move into the house."

She was sorry.

~~~~~~~~~~~~~~~~

The Move to San Francisco

All of my potential helpers were busy with Christmas, but one man I worked with was going to bring his teenage son to help unload the furniture. We had trouble with the truck and were late getting to the apartment. By then they had other commitments, after all it was Christmas Eve, so it was just Jason and me. The truck broke down several times, it was a disaster. I finally had to call some movers from the Delancey Street Rehabilitation Group because we couldn't finish the job alone.

Bett worked down the street and met someone of interest at work. She was going to spend Christmas Day with him and his mother. Jason invited me to spend Christmas with him and his family. I asked if there was room for Bett and he said his aunt didn't have room for one more person. I felt bad and was depressed for the rest of the day. It was not a merry Christmas.

Before Christmas, I asked Jason if he wanted a gift or a memory for his present, and he chose the memory. I made reservations in Carmel for New Year's Eve as his Christmas and birthday gift since his birthday was January 2nd. We had a little cottage with a fireplace that was close to town so we could go out for walks to town and on the beach. For his birthday, I took him to brunch before we returned to reality. It was such a romantic weekend. We always talked about doing this again.

When I moved to the city I gave the car back to my

former broker at the real estate office. By then it was on its last leg. I had put money into it to keep it going, so in addition to making the monthly payment, I was also making repairs. The previous drivers had not taken care of the maintenance required so that caused many problems. I will always be grateful for the use of the car, how it came to me in my time of need, and I only had to tell one person. Since I was in walking distance of work and church the only time I needed a car was to pick up Brit and Case, and Bett let me use her car occasionally when I was in a pinch.

Bett was renting a room from a friend and her husband in Daly City. Jake, her new love, and the couple she lived with planned a surprise birthday party for her. I had directions to the party, but after driving around in circles for about an hour, gave up and came home. Jake called and wanted to know what happened to us. I told him I had a hard time driving the car because it was stick shift and after driving for an hour had come back home. He drove over and picked us up and took us to the party. Jake had planned this party for her and tried to keep her busy until everyone had time to get off work and get to the event. He just wanted to make her happy.

I had hoped that by moving to the city I would be closer to Brit and Case, and I would be able to see them during the week when they weren't with me. I looked at schools in the area and there was a Lutheran school just across the street from my apartment. We visited the school and both of them liked the school and were enthusiastic about living with me. I wanted them to have the experience of growing up in a multi-ethnic school, since I had grown up in Washington, DC, and felt this would better prepare them for life. In the suburbs there wasn't the racial mix like there was in San Francisco. The only bad thing was I couldn't send them out to play like I could in Walnut Creek, and I had to always be with them, watching them. There were parks in the area we could walk to and other children for them to play with, and on weekends many places to go in the city. Greg did not like the idea of them going to school in the city. He had come from a small town in California and didn't think his children should grow up in San Francisco. So, their living with me in the city was not going to happen.

Since my apartment was close to work it was nice to be able to come home for lunch. I found, unfortunately, that once I was home I became too relaxed and didn't want to go back to work. One thing I liked was I was able to have everyone from the office over for lunch to show them my apartment. It was a simple meal of onion soup and salad. I also did a happy hour after work to show off my apartment to co-workers at the other offices. Living in the suburbs, my neighbors were mostly married with children living at home. I felt that I fit in more in the city since I was alone a great deal of the time. My sister came up from Fresno and we did the usual tourist things. I changed churches since I thought I was going to be here for a couple of years. Then I received a call from my tenants saying they were going to be moving. They had only been in the house for six months. I told them if they advertised and found a new tenant that I would let them out of the lease.

I decided I needed to buy a little car to get me to the

grocery store and be able to pick up Brit and Case, because I was not going to be able to depend on Greg's help. I made several trips back to Walnut Creek to interview prospective tenants. I orally accepted a contract from one prospective tenant and the real estate agent brought the lease to my office for me to sign. I signed the contract but did not make a copy. When I received the contract back it had been changed by the tenant or the agent, but the change had not been relayed to me. It wasn't until I later asked an attorney in the office to look at the contract that he pointed this out. When I questioned the agent about this, she had her client find another place. I interviewed another couple, but was not comfortable with them due to their pets in the house and the cats litter box that could leak through to the carpet. After that I decided to move back to Walnut Creek since I was having a difficult time finding the right tenant.

The car I bought while I was living in city had no air conditioning and so I started looking for another car. I sent in for pre-approved credit with one of the big lenders and used my married name. The credit report came back not approved. I decided to submit another application and use my former married name to see how my credit looked. The credit report came back I had been approved and could go down and pick out the car I wanted. This was the deciding factor for me to use my former married name since my credit had been established before I married Greg. I used this time to go car shopping. I wanted a new car that would be appropriate for showing property in case I decided to go back into real estate. I was mainly interested in keeping the price down and finally settled on a four-door model with a four-cylinder engine. I remember I picked the same car my friend had. I decided since her husband worked for the manufacturer and she had this model it must be a good car. I wanted something that was economical on gas and decided on the four cylinders. I remember Brit saying whenever she fell asleep and woke up she wasn't sure if she was in her dad's car or mine since we both had blue interior. It seemed ironic that I financed my car from the same company that repossessed my car previously.

I advertised my Honda for sale and left it on the street a few blocks from my house with a for sale sign. I went by to check on it and drove it occasionally to keep the battery charged and discovered someone had broken into it and tried to steal it, but they just bungled the job. I eventually had to have the car towed to the dealership to be repaired. I sold the car for what I paid and I was able to use it for almost a year, so I considered it was a good buy. Before I sold the car, I had a call from the DMV since the car was over ten years old and the mileage was unusually low. The dealer who sold me the car said that an older couple owned the car and didn't use it often so the mileage was low. A friend that worked for the police department said the dealer was suspected of moving back the odometer on autos he sold.

I told Greg now that I was back in the house Brit and Case could attend school in Walnut Creek. He did not want to let them come back now. I had to petition the court to have them returned to me for the following school year. I represented myself because by then I had no faith in attorneys. I felt I could express myself better than an attorney. We were to go through Contra Costa

Mediation with the court's social service. When I was interviewed by the social worker she dozed off during our meeting. When I went into court I told the judge of that incident. He had the bailiff call her over to the court.

She was sworn in and the judge asked her, "Did you doze off during the meeting?" She said she had not dozed off during our discussion. It was left at that, she was believed over me. Why did the judge think she was going to admit the truth? Sometime later a bailiff from the court told me she was an evil woman, causing a lot of problems for families. She said the reason I don't go into therapy is because I don't want to ruin my relationship with my mother. I wonder what her relationship with her mother was.

I told the court that Greg was a good father, and I knew he would not let anyone hurt them. They would be fed and clothed well, but his main purpose in having custody was to punish me, because I made him take responsibility for them when he didn't want to. While they were with him he kept saying, "When are you going to take them." When I was back in my house and wanted to have them for the following school year he didn't want to let them return. He resented paying me any child support. I had to constantly call him and ask where the check was. We continually argued over how much he owed me and when. The judge listened to me, but did not agree with me and ruled that Brit and Case would remain with me for the summers and with their dad when in school. Greg told the court that I didn't call Case on his birthday. It didn't dawn on me to tell the court we had already celebrated his birthday when he was with me. We celebrated birthdays and holidays according to the calendar set up by the court, so we had to be flexible for important days in their life. When I called my children many times I was told they were asleep, or weren't home and left messages. I didn't call as much because I knew he would make it hard for me to talk to them if he was feeling vindictive. I went to several attorneys to have this decision reversed but finally decided it was going to take a lot of money and would end up dragging me down more. I decided to use a philosophy that one of my babysitter's mother had, "If you think it's a problem, then it's a problem, but if you don't think it's a problem then it's not a problem." I knew there must be a reason why this was to be. I knew one day Greg would want to move out of the area and he would not be able to take them out of the state without my permission.

CHAPTER TWELVE

Ge

When I moved back to the house Ge was one of my first roommates. He was going to be married soon and this was just to be temporary. I didn't really like to have temporary arrangements, but because of my large house payment and all of the other expenses I decided to take him. His girlfriend was a regular visitor, and she would come to my house regularly as soon as she was off work. I could hear them taking showers together since my room backed up to their bathroom. I told him when I rented to him I didn't expect his girlfriend would be visiting every day. Since she lived at home with her parents, they used his room for their romantic get-togethers.

Ad and Her Son

Ad had been living in Walnut Creek and the owner of the townhouse she was renting wanted to have possession. She wanted to stay in Walnut Creek, but couldn't afford her own place when she answered my ad. She rented two rooms, one for herself and one for her son. She was going to school for her master's degree and her son was in a private Catholic high school in the honors program. Since she smoked our agreement was that she would smoke outside. That became a problem when the weather was nice the doors and windows were open in both the front and the back of the house and you could still smell the smoke. She also cut hair for extra income and at times she would have individuals in the kitchen cutting their hair. I told her repeatedly she needed to find another place to cut hair. She could use the deck outside, or in the garage, and then hair wouldn't get all over the place. We had a few words on this matter and then she decided to move. I think she resented me telling her what to do, and also that she was in the position where she had to rent a room. When she wanted her deposit back I told her after all the utility bills were in then I would return her deposit. As it was we went to small claims court over the deposit. She got up in front of the judge and said we didn't have an agreement to split the utility bills and she was entitled to her deposit back. I knew then that she talked to an attorney, and he told her if we didn't have an agreement in writing then it wasn't enforceable. It was then that I put utilities to be split in the contract. She would read her Bible and go to church, but got up in front of the judge and lied in court all for fifty dollars. She also said that her son babysat and he should have been paid. I left for work at 5:30 a.m. and the babysitter came at 6:30 a.m. Brit and Case would still be asleep so he wasn't really babysitting. During the summer, I had two sisters who took turns babysitting and this was the earliest they could be at the house since their mother dropped them off on her way to work. I asked Ad if her son would be at home until this time and she said yes, he would be there. No mention was ever made of any payment for his time since he was still asleep also. I never depended on my roommates to babysit. I would never leave my children with any of them, except if I thought they were extremely dependable and responsible.

〰〰〰〰〰

Ann and Her Daughter

Ann and her daughter A moved from the Midwest, and lived in an apartment in downtown Walnut Creek. After they had been there for a few weeks they found it was just a party area. There was drinking, fighting and noise during the day and long into the evening. She said the police were continually coming to the complex. She was afraid there were drugs being sold in the area, and wanted to be in a safer area. She moved in and rented two rooms for herself and her daughter. She worked at the courthouse in downtown Oakland not knowing this was a high crime area. Evidently, she had taken the job without seeing the area and was concerned for her safety going to and coming from work. She especially didn't like the comments she received when going past a group of men. She wasn't happy with her job and her friends and family continued to call her to encourage her to return home. We had gone out a couple of times together to the singles dances and other get-togethers, but she hadn't met anyone. One week before she was to move back to family she met someone at one of the dances. They went out for the evening and she didn't come home until after lunch. It was a good thing Ho and I were there or A would have been left alone I am sure. Ho was usually home with his daughter who he had custody of, so he and I watched after A. Ann stayed in her room a great deal watching soap operas on the television. When my children were with me it made a great play group for the girls, and sometimes Case when he wanted to join them. Ann and I could make plans to go out in the evening, as Ho was always there with his daughter. We knew he would not allow any roughhousing, and could be quite strict, as he was an ex-Marine. He would give them breakfast if we weren't up in the morning, but most of the time they would wait for me because he was a vegetarian. They hadn't acquired the taste for his veggie burgers and artificial eggs for breakfast as his daughter had. A had a habit of trying to play his daughter against Brit. I didn't know how to handle it and tried to just watch from a distance. Sometimes I tried to divert their attention to some other activity. I didn't always handle the problem as well as I could have. One time I got angry at Brit when she started crying because A excluded her from their play time. I tried to protect Brit but I know sometimes A was cruel. Before they moved I planted azaleas next to the sidewalk. After they left I noticed all of them had been broken. I always thought it was A who did that. I also was missing some knickknacks after they left. I think she was carrying around a lot of anger maybe because she didn't have a family life like other children in school. When she was ten, she asked her mother who her father was, and wanted to meet him. Ann had not told A's father about her birth, and raised A on her own. Ann said it was a big surprise to him when she called him, and told him he had a daughter and she was ten. The first thing he said was that he didn't have any money, thinking that was the reason for the visit. It was a relief to see A go. I hope she is happy now.

~~~~~~~~~~

Ho, His Son and Daughter

Ho was a Vietnam veteran. He married a Vietnam-ese woman and had two children with her. Ho took over raising their daughter, who was only four, when he moved into my house. His son was living with his mother in Southern California, but when he became too difficult for her to manage she sent him to Ho. Ho was self-employed as a plumber and because he received payment in cash a lot of times he put a lock on his door. He was the first roommate to put a lock on his door. No one else was ever concerned about their privacy or anyone going into their room. Ho's girlfriend survived cancer by going to a clinic in Tijuana. They were both vegetarians and she survived by juicing organic carrots, eating raw calves' liver and coffee enemas. When my sister developed cancer, I talked to her about this treatment, but she wanted to stay with the traditional method of chemotherapy and radiation after she had a double mastectomy. He always paid me in cash because he said he didn't have a bank account. I preferred to be paid in check because it was easier for me to use the automatic teller rather than going into the bank during normal banking hours. Even though he was a plumber it was seldom that he did any repair work for me. I guess when he was home he didn't want to be called on for any jobs. He always made sure his daughter was fed and had clean clothes, but at dinner time he would take his homemade soup into the family room to eat, and leave her at the table by herself. I know when my children were there or A was around she was much happier. She missed her mother and showed us pictures of her. She didn't see her mother in the time they were with me. When her brother came to stay he slept on the floor in his sister's room. After Ann left I told Ho he could rent another room for his son, but he didn't want to do that and instead rented a house and moved. His son was not having an easy readjustment and would get into fights at school, coming home with his face bloodied and bruised. He was very helpful when I needed help around the house, and I tried to help him know how much I appreciated what he did.

<hr>

Em and Her Daughter

Em had just moved from out of state for a new job due to a promotion. She originally brought her daughter and son to California, but her son returned home to live with his dad as he wasn't happy. Em was going to rent two rooms eventually but only took one room in the beginning. I later realized she didn't want the expense of two rooms when she and her daughter could sleep together and had the use of the entire house otherwise.

She was helpful and cheerful. She never expected me to be the perfect parent or spouse she never had. She was a concerned mother. She did go out on Fridays to the western bar down the road and sometimes had dents on her car the next day, which I never asked about nor did she ever explain. I thought the place she went to had a reputation as being a rough crowd, but that was the type of atmosphere she liked. I am sure she was lonely after the move, and since she was about forty to fifty pounds overweight this was the type of place she felt comfortable. She helped me with the housework, as at the time I had two other male roommates. They made the offer for all of us to share the cooking. She and I cooked the first meal and we all ate together. Then it was their turn to cook and for some reason they weren't able to take their turn. After the second time we did the cooking we finally realized that they were not going to take their turn cooking. They liked us to be the cooks. Jo had come to live here after breaking up with his girlfriend. He was quiet, and didn't do much cooking. When he came home in the evening he usually went to his room and meditated, then out for dinner. His job was somewhat unstable as an engineer, and he was worried about being laid off. After he helped me repair a broken sprinkler he left the sprinkler pipe still exposed and did not finish the job by putting the plastic pipe back in the ground. I wondered if he did the same sloppy work for his employer. He tried to help occasionally, especially if he wanted to have overnight guests. I had an empty room and for some reason my roommates figured that they could invite their friends over to spend the night and use my extra room. I finally had to let them know it was not available. Ra was also living in the house at the same time. When he moved in I loaned him a bed, along with blankets and sheets. After he bought a bed he neglected to return my linens. I guess he forgot they didn't belong to him. He was in the process of getting a divorce after leaving his wife because she did not want to work and help him with the expenses. She didn't mind working part-time in a dead-end job, but she was not interested in a career. Their son was somewhat of a problem when he was visiting. Ra would take a nap and thought because there were females in the house he didn't have to watch his son. His son was not an easy child to handle, as he was very hyper. One night his son was taking a bath and I heard the water splashing over the tub on the floor. I told Ra he needed to go up to the bathroom and get him out. His son could not do that. It would ruin the floor and it was impossible to dry out the carpet in the bathroom after it was soaked. I always had a problem with that bathroom. The shower curtains didn't seem to keep the water in the tub. I was continually fixing the bathroom walls, recaulking the tub and shower area. I was always looking for towel racks that would have space for everyone's towel so that the bathroom didn't look so bad.

Ra and Jo decided to move out together and rent an apartment. They thought their romantic life would improve if they had their own apartment so they could bring women home. They knew I did not like to have a lot of strange people overnight in my house. Before they moved they took me out for dinner. It was a fun evening. We went to dinner in Berkeley and afterwards went to the movie, *The Rocky Horror Show*. I had never seen such sights in a movie theatre. People were dressed in costumes, throwing popcorn, food and water. It was an experience. After they moved Jo came back to visit. I think he missed us. He brought some clothing for one of my roommates to mend, since he didn't know how to sew. He said Ra wanted to do the bills the same way I did. I just charged a flat rate and paid all the utility bills myself. Jo didn't want to go along with that. Ra did meet someone and they were going to get married. He found someone who wanted a career and marriage, and she would help him to reach the financial goals he wanted to achieve.

CHAPTER THIRTEEN

Bett's Wedding

Em was there to help me with the dinner I was planning for my daughter's wedding. The wedding was in a garden setting in Marin. Bett wanted to have a band and was also planning on appetizers and champagne. Her father and I were paying the costs. Her mother-in-law to be had given her a book that said the bride's family paid for the wedding, even though her mother-in-law invited most of her friends. I received only three invitations my daughter mailed. It was a very stressful time for us. Bett and I went shopping for the wedding dress and I paid for half. The dress she chose was on the front of the latest bridal magazine. I later told her I was not going to be able to give her as much as I planned because I was paying for Prip and my niece to come out for the wedding. My mother told me Prip was sick but I didn't realize how sick. Prip did not want to tell me that she had cancer and was undergoing chemotherapy. My sisters told me they thought I was not strong enough to handle such bad news after all the court cases I had gone through due to divorce and custody issues. I guess that was the way my family handled things, keeping secrets. Later, when she told me she had cancer I told her about a cancer therapy group in Tijuana we could go to. She said she didn't have money and would have to go where her insurance was going to pay. I told her we would find the money somehow if she wanted to pursue this avenue. She was not interested. I always felt that Prip was going to die of cancer. I would die of a heart attack, but she would die of cancer. She was always trying to be happy, keeping everything inside and not sharing any of her concerns. I hesitated asking her for help sometimes because I felt she did favors because she didn't know how to say no. When she moved to Oklahoma she had never been away from family, or lived on her own. She always lived with family or her husband. After the death of her son, I felt she was never able to really grieve and didn't have the family support that she needed. Her husband was not able to give her the support she needed and retreated into his own cocoon. I am sure it was tragic for him as well, since he had lost his father, then his step-father, and now his son to an unexpected death. I told her before she moved to Oklahoma if she found a church in the area that she liked it would be a great help to her.

She said, "But you belonged to a church and look how bad things were for you."

I told her, "But think of how much worse they could have been if I didn't have the help and support of my Pastor and the church members."

That convinced her to find a church and it did help her greatly in her time of need.

After I told Bett I wasn't going to be giving her as much financial help she and her dad were angry at me. He said he would pay for everything and hoped I didn't show my face at the wedding.

She was spending a great deal of money and kept saying, "But this is my only wedding, I will only do this once."

Since she and Jake had been living together already she didn't think she should be paying for the wedding, that it was still her father's and my responsibility. Her maid of honor was her best friend, who had been her friend since first grade.

I arranged to use the van from the vanpool and drove to the San Francisco airport to pick up Prip and my niece for the wedding. Her husband decided not to come because of work. I went to the airport and her plane was delayed because of thunderstorms. I drove back home since I had all the kids and was told by the airline that it could be a long wait. When I got back to the house I heard my mother on the phone say, "Well she should be there soon." Prip just arrived and I had to turn around and go back to the airport and pick her up. It was a shock when I saw her to see how short her hair was. She lost a lot of hair and Lynn had cut it very short to make it look neater. I then had to drive to San Jose to pick up my son and grandson for the wedding. Later that evening, my sister and her husband arrived from Fresno with my dad who had never been to my house. We were all going to stay at my house, something we had not done since I was seven years old. I felt this was going to be our last opportunity, especially now with Prip's cancer treatment. I don't know how long she had cancer since they just told me, but I was sure she would survive and we would have plenty of celebrations together. My dad was to sleep in the family room on the couch and my mother in the living room on the hide-a-bed. My sisters and niece would be upstairs in the extra bedroom. After dinner, my sister Lynn said she was going to spend the night at her friend's house and was taking our niece with her. I told her I spent a lot of money for us all to stay together. She left anyway. The next morning, I had bagels and juice for everyone to have before we left for the wedding. Lynn didn't make it to my house until late and didn't get a chance to eat. When we arrived for the pictures and taking care of last minute details for the wedding, Lynn took Prip and our niece to get something to eat. Later when the wedding took place I didn't see her in the group, but I saw her dress through the trees, and Prip and Nk were with her. They had their backs to the ceremony. I thought it was rude and disrespectful, but decided not to let this ruin my day. The wedding was wonderful. We had a great time. I drove everyone over the Golden Gate Bridge and through San Francisco so they could see some of the town. When we got back home I had to take the van back and fill it with gas.

The next day mother, Prip, Lynn, our niece and I went into San Francisco to see the city while they were visiting. We had a picture taken at one of the studios where we dressed up in old-fashioned clothes. After we returned, mother and I were in the kitchen by ourselves and I told her I was taking everyone to the train station a day early. My dad was driving me crazy. He kept flipping the television channels. He couldn't get the coffee hot enough and I had to constantly run to the store for more milk and juice for him. I had run out of food. I guess I didn't realize how much it would take to feed everyone for this period of time. They all seemed to just sit and expect me to wait on them for everything, even for a glass of water, they couldn't get that for themselves. After I waited on everyone and fixed dinner my last time I told my sister Lynn and my dad that I was taking them to the train station in the morning. In the morning when I went in to tell Lynn it was time to leave, she became angry. She got in the car with my mom and dad and everyone started arguing. I said if they did not stop I would call a cab for them to get to the train station. Lynn said she was never going to come to my house again. My dad kept saying you are sisters, you are not supposed to act like this. I told Lynn I had paid for Prip and our niece to attend this wedding and I resented the fact that she went to her friend's house to spend the night and took our niece, when they were here for such a short time. When the vows were said I could see them off in another area. She said she was not feeling well, that her stomach was upset. I left them at the train station and went back home. Prip was still asleep. I cleaned house and then woke them up so we could go do something. We went to Jack London Square for lunch and then Prip wanted to take her daughter shopping. I told her the stores in Walnut Creek were expensive and we could go to Concord to shop, but she wanted to shop there. I guess Lynn had given her money to shop. The next day I took them to the airport and never did get a thank you from either of them. I waited for a letter and nothing came and I finally wrote a letter expressing my anger over their behavior at my daughter's wedding. Prip did not respond. I was angry that I paid for them to come to San Francisco and they were not even present for the wedding. Later, I read a book someone from work loaned me about sisters and a falling out these sisters had over a daughter's wedding. I sent the book to Prip to read and enclosed a stamped self-addressed envelope for her to send the book back, but she did not return the book. I wrote her several times and finally a letter was returned to me marked "refused" on the envelope in my sister's handwriting. I bought my friend another copy of the book and told her that I lost her copy. I didn't try to correspond with her after that, she made her feelings known. I know my sister Lynn read the letter because my mother said she made a comment about it.

~~~~~~~~~

Prip's Death: *December 1987*

I joined a women's therapy group at Kaiser that met weekly while I was going through the custody battle. My mother told me Prip was in the hospital and our dad said he was going to see her when Lynn left. I told him that Lynn was staying until the end. If he wanted to go he should go now. I called to talk to her and hadn't been able to get through to her, as the nurses had just given her a shot for pain and she was not awake.

When I picked up Brit and Case for the weekend I told them Prip was still in the hospital.

Case said, "Good, then, that means she hasn't died."

I called one night and they had just given her a shot

for the pain and she was drowsy. The nurse put the phone up to her so we could talk. I told her I was sorry for our estrangement and the part I played, and that I loved her and she told me the same thing.

My mother said, "Don't call."

I don't know why she would tell me not to call her, since we didn't know whether it would be our last conversation. I was so glad we were able to talk even if it was just a short time. We hadn't talked since my daughter's wedding, and I sent her "the letter." I called almost every day before Christmas. Christmas Eve Brit, Case, and I called just to tell her we loved her. We weren't able to talk very long because of the pain medications she had been given, but we were able to say hello, Merry Christmas, and we loved her. Whenever the phone rang I thought it was the hospital or someone calling to tell me she had died. Christmas Day came and she was still hanging on. The day after Christmas I came home from work exhausted and laid down on the couch to rest and watch the news. The phone rang several times, but no one left a message. It rang again and no one left a message. I finally realized someone was trying to reach me and I decided I better answer the phone. It was Lynn. I knew she was calling to tell me, Prip was gone. We knew it was coming, but it was very, very sad. We wouldn't be able to see her again, to talk and laugh like we once did. We only had our memories of how much fun we had when we were together.

I went to work the next day and dug in taking all of the Christmas decorations down, as physical activity helped release some of the tension. I went to my therapy group but didn't want to be the first one to share. I waited until everyone had a chance to talk about where they were in their life and then told them of my sister dying the day after Christmas. The therapy group was the only one I said anything to except for my two roommates.

When I left work, I didn't tell anyone about the death of my sister. I didn't want to start crying, and I didn't know when we would have the funeral since my sister's body was being shipped from Oklahoma. I didn't want to tell Bett on the phone about Prip's death since we were going to Soda Springs after Christmas. I didn't expect her to call mother, who told her about Prip's passing. She was upset with me for not telling her sooner. I thought it would be better to wait while we were all together. We rented a townhouse, and I was hoping this would be a better time to talk about her passing. Luckily, she is a very forgiving person. I preferred staying there because the downhill skiing was in walking distance and I could go cross-country skiing close by. I took Brit and Case for lessons for cross-country skiing, thinking this would be easier for them. I was hoping they would like it, and we would be able to do this together because I didn't like downhill skiing. They were in front of me on the skiing path after their lesson, but Case got impatient and wanted to take a shortcut, so he took off across the field.

I heard the man in front of me say, "Who is watching that boy?"

He was lucky he didn't sink in over his head in the snow. I had to take off after him to help him, but he was too fast for me. After that I knew this was not something they wanted to do again, but he now likes cross-country skiing better than downhill because it is so peaceful and less crowds. Brit tried downhill a couple of times at Tahoe when we went to the Presbyterian family resort for another Christmas. She froze at the top of the ski lift the last time we went when we were in Fresno, and had to make it down very slowly. After that she never tried downhill again. No matter what we did it was so nice being together with the rest of the family and where they could enjoy the other activities in the snow.

After Prip's death I said to my mother, "It's too bad the baby she had before Nk was born didn't live because then Nk would have a sister now."

Mother told me, "The baby lived, but she gave it up for adoption and told everyone that it had died."

I think that was too much of a burden for her to handle all those years. Only Lynn knew and she hadn't told me anything about the adoption. After Prip's son Ro died when he was only three years old, she developed breast cancer. I think when she gave up one child for adoption and then lost another child at a very young age, a large hole was left in her heart. She probably grieved over the years for the child she had given up and to keep that a secret was too much to hold in.

Bett, her husband and I drove to Fresno for the funeral. It was not easy to see her in the casket. I didn't want to go into the viewing room, but could see from outside the room that she was wearing a wig. My dad didn't go into the viewing room either. Later I learned that by not viewing the body of a loved one, it takes longer for the brain to process their death and that they are no longer alive.

My dad had been in a coma for six weeks due to an aneurism of the abdomen, and when he returned home he said Patty Duke came to him in his dreams. He couldn't understand why that happened. I told him that wasn't Patty Duke, that was Prip, our sister, but he didn't recognize her because of the wig she wore when she was buried. One of the reasons I don't fear death, is because I know I will be with Prip, our mother, and grandmother.

~~~~~~~~~

Bett and Jake

I felt so relieved that Bett was married to someone so caring and understanding. I didn't have to worry about her anymore. It was a great relief to know she was happy, secure and safe. She and Jake worked together, and he bought the house they were going to live in while they were still engaged. They started fixing it up with a modern kitchen, painting and new carpets. He was handy around the house and was able to do a lot of things himself. He was so handy that other people also called him to help on their house projects. I'm sure he was taken advantage of a lot because he probably never said no to anyone.

Once when I asked for him to help me on my house, Bett said, "I wish you helpless women would stop calling my husband to help with your homes."

He helped his mother take care of her house because she was alone also. She was older than I was and didn't do much in repairs on her house, just letting it go until it was at the emergency stage. I tried to fix things when they became an emergency or an "A" repair. The "B" repairs didn't get fixed unless they were an emergency stage. Plumbing and electrical had to be fixed immediately. Jake came over to patch my roof in one spot where water damaged the ceiling in the end bedroom. It only took him probably an hour but then the drive was an hour over and an hour back. I always had a barbeque and we could go swimming so it was more like a family event. I always thought he would do anything for Bett to make her happy, and how blessed she was.

Bett suggested we go to Tahoe and rent a cabin for the coming Christmas, and I was invited along with her husband's mother. We all shared in the cost and would be cooking our meals at the cabin. We went up Christmas Eve and I was to pick up Brit and Case on Christmas Day. It was great at the cabin and in the morning we had eggs benedict and then I went to pick up my children. This was not something I was looking forward to. This was not the way it was supposed to be. Me standing outside knocking on the door to pick my children up, when before I was always greeted with open arms. I waited outside for them while they got their things together. I am sure this was not easy for them either. The transition from one house to another was difficult. Brit's bed was the same bed at my house that she had at her dad's house. He had taken one of the beds we bought for my older children, and I kept one. I hated to leave Tahoe as I planned on driving to Walnut Creek so the kids could open their presents there. It was awful being in Walnut Creek by myself. I don't know why I didn't drive back up to the cabin. I guess I didn't know how beautiful the weather was going to be. Holidays were difficult for us in Walnut Creek. It was so lonely. Everyone I knew was busy with their family and if I didn't go to Fresno or Southern California we had no one. If my family couldn't come to me then I would go to them. The court set the schedule that I would have Christmas or Christmas Eve with my children, and it would alternate each year.

CHAPTER FOURTEEN

Cy

Cy was looking for a safe haven from a divorce also. I didn't know it at the time but Br told me after she moved that she kept a gun in her room. I thought if someone has to keep a gun in their room because they didn't feel safe, then they should live someplace else. She was a quiet, clean person. She had her own phone put in her room. She didn't socialize much, just went to work, came home, and visited with her family. After a couple of months, she decided she needed to be on her own. I was sorry to see her leave, until I found out she had the gun. She was escaping an abusive marriage and thought she needed a gun in case he found out where she lived and came looking for her. She spent a lot of time in her room and it was usually very warm upstairs until the sun went down. I don't know how she could stand the heat, or to be cooped up in a small room. She probably moved on the spur of the moment and my home was available.

Ja and Her Children

Ja moved in saying that her two sons, ages two and four, would be staying with their father at his mother's. They would be visiting occasionally. She worked for an attorney's office and seemed quiet and clean. The first night she moved in, her sons and her husband came over and she fixed them dinner, bathed her sons and they all spent the night in her room. The next night her boyfriend came over and when I went to work in the morning his motorcycle was still in the driveway. She told me it had broken down. I told her I thought she needed her own place and would give her a week to find another place. She became indignant and wrote me nasty letters stating what her rights were and how she would sue me. I figured she received advice from the attorneys at her work. It was stressful until she moved, but I managed to keep my comments to myself. I think she took the room for herself, but planned all along on having her husband and sons staying with her. She knew I would not rent to her if there were going to be three other people in the room. I am sure the story she gave me was just to get in the house.

Jh the Magician

Jh was a magician who worked on a cruise ship before moving into my home. He had been raised in the Midwest with a very conservative family. He graduated from college, but decided to become a magician. He just returned from a cruise where he was part of the entertainment. He met a teacher on the cruise who lived in Danville, and moved to Walnut Creek to be closer to her. She did not want to entertain him in her house with her daughter home, so she would come and visit with him in his room. I knew she was there when I saw her car outside and his bedroom door was shut. It was summer and I don't know how they could stand it in his room with the heat, since that side of the house received the evening sun. I never did see what she looked like. I just saw her car outside. I wondered how she could behave this way, my roommates and I had children in the house. It was very uncomfortable for me fixing dinner when his bedroom was just above the kitchen. When he moved in he needed a place for his pigeons and rabbits outside in the garage. He put on a magic show for us, and it was great. I invited some people from church for the magic show, but they weren't able to come. When Brit held his rabbit and stroked his soft fur I saw her eyes soften and I knew I had to have a rabbit for her. Before he moved he built a rabbit hutch for us. We named her Peaches because she was the color of my carpet, and she lived seven years mainly due to Br taking such good care of her. We would bring her in the house, but it was hard to catch her unless we had carrots with the green top. I would call to her and show her the carrot and she would go back under my bed and then come out again until she couldn't resist the carrot. We had a funeral in the back yard for her when she died, and I thought it was such a beautiful way to be remembered.

He was such a gentle man. He reminded me of a modern-day John the Baptist. When his van showed up and he got out with his long dark hair and his beard my first impression was, oh no. After I talked to him I decided to give him a try. I'm sure my neighbors didn't like his van in the driveway, but he had props in the van for his magic show that he needed to protect. I don't think the relationship with his new friend worked out so he was going back to working for the cruise lines. I guess after he took off his tuxedo and left the cruise ship the reality hit them both and they lost the magic they had. He was such a nice person, it's too bad his girlfriend didn't know what a good thing she had.

~~~~~~~~~

Br and Her Daughter

Br called me a year before she moved in, but because she didn't have a car she was never able to come and meet me. Her brother brought her to see the room, and she liked it and wanted to move in as soon as she could. They wanted me to lower my price, explaining she was on welfare and had a small child to support, and asked if I could take less.

I said no.

I thought I was being very reasonable with my prices. Br and Ma lived in one room because that was all they could afford, so they were getting a bargain price. I told her she could put some of her things in the garage and if she had anything to put in the family room she could. At first, she had a wicker basket and a bench she left in the family room. She worried about the wear and tear it was going to take in the family room. I don't know how it was going to be ruined since no one ever sat on either, but she had these concerns. I needed a vacuum cleaner and I knew she had a couple in her room and asked if we could borrow one of them. I had gone through several and had them repaired numerous times. I couldn't understand how she could have room for three vacuums in her room, but I soon realized that she was a hoarder. She saved everything including all of the papers her daughter did in school. When I became aware of some of the things in the garage she was saving, along with empty boxes, I told her we didn't have room for them. I was trying to keep the garage from being a place to store junk. If I was going to put the house on the market later I needed to be able to keep the garage somewhat neat and clean.

Br was a great help to me in keeping the house clean. She liked to cook and was home all day so she usually kept the kitchen clean. Since she did her cooking during the day while I was at work it was usually no problem, but later she became more and more of a recluse and did her cooking late at night. At times I would come home from being out and she was baking at midnight. When I moved into the room next to her and she was in the kitchen I had to go downstairs and tell her she was making too much noise and 2:00 a.m. was not the time to cook. I commented to her once that she and I were like family because we ended up living together over seven years.

Her daughter was a very shy, sensitive little girl and because she missed a great deal of school she almost didn't get promoted to first grade. I think Br encouraged her daughter's illnesses so Ma would stay home from school to keep her company. Otherwise, she had no purpose. Br's brother bought her a bike because she didn't have a car, and needed a way to get around. She usually took the bus and did her errands, but with the bike she had baskets on the side for her groceries. I wanted her to babysit for me, but because she was on AFDC she wasn't able to work and take money or else she would lose her funding. It seemed strange in the summer when Brit and Case were with me I would have to pay a babysitter even though she was in the house. She said she wasn't able to get them to behave and couldn't maintain control, so they took advantage of her good nature. She would retreat to her room and shut the door in order to cope when things got out of control with them.

Twice a year I would move all of the furniture outside and clean the carpets and she was always there to help me.

Once I said to her daughter, "Aren't you glad you don't have to do this?"

She said she thought it was fun, everyone working together to get the house clean, the camaraderie and joint effort. Whenever Br baked she would always share her goodies with my children. We didn't eat together because she was a vegetarian and ate a lot of tofu. She made special dishes for her daughter from recipes she found in the library. These foods were marketed to make individuals smarter and able to concentrate on their lessons. She was hoping this would help Ma in school, so she wouldn't get held back.

At other times she would tell her, "You'll never be good at math. I was never good at it either."

I didn't know if Br graduated from college, but her father was a surgeon in the military so she came from an educated family, but something made her give up on life.

She said that when her daughter was born she took the money she inherited from her dad and used that for the same hospital room Cher had when she delivered her child. While she lived with me she had little contact with others except her mother and her brother. Her mother would pick her up on Saturdays to come and clean for her, and then brought them back at the end of the day unless there was a very big project that took longer. Ma said that her grandmother didn't treat Br very well. I enjoyed talking with Br's mother while Br was getting her things together. I am sure she was grateful they both lived in a nice, safe neighborhood with good schools.

I think some of our problems were because I reminded her of her mother. I knew when I talked to her I needed to use my most gentle voice, otherwise she was going to run upstairs to her room and shut the door and wouldn't come out until after I had gone to bed or to work. It was not easy living with that treatment, but I tried to overlook it most times, since I was really grateful for her help.

When the neighbors across the street wanted her to babysit, she agreed, but they were going to pay her with food and other necessities. She preferred to sit for them in my home so she could bake while they were there. That became a problem for me when I came home to study for my securities exam and they were there in the house, practicing their violin and flute lessons. I finally told her she couldn't sit for them in my house, she needed to go to their house. I needed my peace and quiet when I came home, and I needed to be able to use the family room for my studying. The mother came over to talk me into letting her babysit in my house.

I still said, "No I need my quiet."

Br decided she didn't like babysitting at their house and she gave up the job. They were never friendly to me after that as they were stuck until they could find other arrangements for their children.

After that Ma got a paper route, but Br was the one who did most of the work, and it was hard work. Usually they would work in the garage, but when it was cold they tried working in the entryway of the house, but they argued so much and got so loud that didn't work out either. The only way they could deliver them was on Br's bike, so they had to make several deliveries. Ma was able to keep the money because AFDC didn't consider that to be Br's income, but many times Ma was still in bed while her mother was doing her work.

I wanted to help Brit and Case become more independent and not be afraid of life, so I took them on the bus and showed them how to get to day camp. I had to leave early in the morning in order to pick them up on time in the evening. By taking public transportation, they could sleep late and not have to rush eating breakfast. That evening I asked them how their ride was, and they said Br rode all the way with them. She was afraid to let them go on the bus alone. I told her Walnut Creek was a safe place, they would be okay. They just had a ride of a few blocks, but she did not want to believe they could do it on their own.

I told her, "I grew up in Washington, DC and took

public transportation all over the city with my two younger sisters. I want them to learn how to use public transportation so they can develop their self-confidence and self-esteem, that they can do things on their own."

Babysitters

During the summers when Brit and Case were with me it was always a challenge to find a babysitter. I asked for referrals from church and friends and found one babysitter who lived close by. She ended up leaving because Brit and Case locked her out of the house. They weren't very nice to her and she ended up taking them home with her to her mother's several times. After that I found GA. Her Mother would bring her in the morning and I would take her home in the evening. They really liked her, but it was probably because she would call her mother and her mother would come and pick them all up and take them to her house. She had a beautiful house. I couldn't believe she wanted to babysit for me. That was the problem living in an upper income neighborhood, no one needed extra spending money, so they weren't willing to do jobs like babysitting. I think GA probably wanted to feel like she was making her own money and being independent. I am sure her mother was proud of her for being able to do this job, because I know it was tough babysitting for them. One time Case bounced his superball in the entryway and broke the chandelier, and she wanted to pay for the damage.

I told her, "No, I know how rambunctious he is, so I don't blame you."

There were many repairs over the years I had to make due to his exuberance, such as the towel racks that he liked to hang on to. I wish I could have found another babysitter like her after she moved. Brit and Case kept saying, "We like GA, we want her back" but she was no longer in the area.

One year before the end of school I called the high school to see if any students were looking for work. I received a call from one girl, and she came for the interview with her mother. Their family was also going through divorce, and the extra income would come in handy for school clothes and supplies. There were four sisters and they usually all came together, so when I got home in the evening the house was usually a mess. They went through my drawers looking to see what kind of things I kept, and I noticed the pennies I used to play card games disappeared. Another time they were doing their nails and spilled nail polish on the carpet. They used nail polish remover to get the nail polish off the carpet which bleached out the color of the carpet. They had to bring their younger sister with them, and she was not easy for them to handle, in addition to my children. I told them the living room was off limits, because of the breakables. The children were running in the living room and when I came home they told me the ceramic giraffe I made had been broken. I told them I was going to take the money out of their pay for the damage since I felt it was due to the younger sister being at my house. I docked them a small amount, and then when I found long distance calls had been made by one of the sisters, I docked that amount also, so that was the last year they babysat. They were angry at me for this, but I felt that was a lesson they needed to learn.

The next summer I ran an ad for a babysitter and only one person answered my ad. I planned on taking Brit and Case to LA with me for a week while I was on an assignment from work. I took the babysitter and her son, which was a free vacation for them. I found a place at Venice Beach and thought this location would give the kids plenty to do with the beach and boardwalk shops to keep themselves busy. I told the babysitter not to use the telephone, if she wanted to make any calls to use the pay phone, and no room service. I gave her money for pizza for lunch. I brought cereal for breakfast and snacks with us, so they had plenty to eat. She was a large African-American and her son was the same age as my daughter. She was very active in her church and said she had a boyfriend, but they were not living together. When I came back to the hotel that night, it was very depressing. When I made the reservations, I didn't know we were in a drug zone and couldn't go out at night and feel safe. The next day I found a large room for us at another hotel, and we moved that day at lunch. It was a lot of hassle and very stressful, but it was worth it. I had taken my mother to this hotel once when I was on an assignment and we really liked it. We knew a lot of movie stars stayed there at one time and could feel their spirits around us. We liked it so much that we didn't even want to go out for dinner, so we would have room service or buy something and bring it back to our room. In the evening it was always a problem to find a place to eat that all of the kids liked. Once we went to Marina Del Rey and Brit couldn't stand the smell of fish, so we left there. Another time we went to a Filipino Restaurant that said they had fried chicken and other American dishes.

When we were seated and looking at the menu Brit said, "Don't they have just plain American food?"

She always asked the waitress, "Do you have homemade dressing for the salad?"

Of course, no one knew what she was talking about. What she wanted was the Italian salad dressing I made at home.

Sometimes before she could ask, Case would say, "Do you have homemade dressing?"

Unfortunately, no one made homemade dressing like mom.

When we returned to Walnut Creek she continued to sit for me. I offered her the job of cooking dinner before she left so she and her son could join us for dinner. She was a good cook, but used way too much salt. It was nice not to have to cook in the evening after a long day and commute.

Brit asked me to teach her how to cook, and I said, "Sure, what would you like to learn how to cook first?" Her response was she wanted to learn how to make play-doh. She knew I made play-doh for my Sunday school class, so that was our first cooking lesson. I don't know if she remembered my recipe for salad dressing, but it was just wine vinegar, salad oil, garlic powder, Italian spices, salt and pepper. She would drink whatever was left in the bowl after the salad was finished, she liked it so much. Later I bought a child's cookbook so we could cook simple things together. We didn't use it very much, but I gave her the book when I went to see her. I told her if you have children, you can teach them how to cook.

CHAPTER FIFTEEN

Ca

Ca answered my ad for a room in my house. When she called to inquire about the room she couldn't talk because she was at work. She asked me to call her back later when she would have some privacy. She didn't have her car so I picked her up at lunch, and she looked at the room that was available. She was contemplating leaving her husband. He had taken her car from her while she was at work and she had to figure a way to get it back so she could get to her job every day. Because I was so close to her work she could walk to work until she could get her car. She moved her things into the room and didn't park her car in front of the house because she didn't want him to know where she lived in case he was driving in the neighborhood looking for her. We became friends and went to the singles dances together. On Mother's Day she fixed dinner for Br and me.

Instead of going to church in Walnut Creek for Mother's Day, my children and I went into San Francisco and attended Glide Memorial Service with the people from the inner city. They had a special day planned for mothers, a free dinner at a restaurant and babysitting for their children. The dinner was meant for people who had no money. One of the ushers told Brit and Case they would have fun if they wanted to join them. There was plenty of food and they probably would have a food fight and play games. I told them no, we would not be participating, but appreciated their kind offer. We were not dressed in our usual church clothes, but had on our jeans and tennis shoes. They probably thought we came for the free dinner for mothers. I decided to do something different this Mother's Day and we had a great day. I bought myself a Chinese tea pot for my Mother's Day present and we had tea with our dinner later at home. Ca liked to entertain and this gave her a chance to shine, since she could not be with her own mother who was in Utah. She stayed with me a couple of months, but decided to move into a friend's house for a very good price. She wanted to have her own place for entertaining and to have quiet, romantic evenings. I knew I was going to miss her company and was sorry to see her go. I tried not to take it personally she was leaving. I knew it was going to cost her a great deal more than she realized with all of the utilities and upkeep on the house, but she was willing to overlook that expense. She met someone at the singles group who would become her husband. When they were married she had the wedding in a Unity Church. They talked to my pastor about getting married there, but he required counseling sessions for a couple of months before he would marry them. They wanted to get married before deer season, or they would have to wait until spring, so all of her family could come to the wedding. The wedding was very nice and the reception was in her backyard. I met Ba at the wedding, who was a colleague of Ca's. He was from Australia and we had a lot to talk about when I told him of my trip to Australia. He didn't know many Americans that had been to as many cities in Australia as I had. I think he was homesick and we went out to dinner occasionally. He became a good friend. After Ca moved we called her room the "marrying room," because anyone who had that room ended up getting married.

<hr />

The Road Less Traveled

I found Scott Peck's book in our church library quite by accident and checked it out so many times that I finally bought my own copy. I also started buying his tapes and listened to them in the car or at night if I had a difficult time sleeping. Brit had given me a tape of his one Christmas. I was touched that she had noticed. I became such an expert on his book I had discussion groups in my home for the singles group. I was surprised so many people came to my sessions, until a couple of the individuals said they were referred to me by their therapist. I told them before I began my discussion that I was not a therapist and this meeting should not take the place of going to therapy. I always recommended they stay in therapy in order to find peace and healing in their life. The singles group had a conference in the spring and the board voted to have Scott Peck as the main speaker. Since I was familiar with his writings I became part of the planning committee. I was able to take time off from work and as I had a four-door sedan, I volunteered to pick him up and return him to the airport. It was a real honor to be able to meet him in person. Because I read his book so many times and listened to his tapes over and over again I felt like we had a special bond.

In his book, he wrote that before he was a psychologist he didn't follow any Christian faith. He changed his opinion after meeting with so many people that survived such horrors in their lives, he knew that the only reason they were still alive was because they were saved by the grace of God. I knew that my sisters and I had only made it because of God's protection in our lives.

Our dad drank when he drove and had several car accidents that we survived. Another time he started a fire in his bedroom when he fell asleep smoking. He was lucky he could jump out his bedroom window onto a porch. Our dog Beanie came into my bedroom and woke me up, or it could have been worse. I don't know who called the fire department because we didn't have a phone. He didn't believe we needed one since there was no one he wanted to talk to, but it was probably more because bill collectors couldn't call him when he was late or didn't pay his bills. If he had been out drinking and had a habit of cooking late at night and falling asleep with oil on the stove for frying. The kitchen floor was burned where he dropped a hot pan when he tried to take it off the stove.

In addition to the discussion groups, I had sing-alongs at church with a potluck afterward. The Presbyterian Church had opened their church to singles in the area for Sunday night events. Their pastor was single and he was not a drinker, so he started the group for other singles. Just about any night of the week there were events for the single individuals. I was able to have my church provide space for events and share some of the load for the singles group.

I was interviewed by the *Lutheran Brotherhood Magazine* regarding my experience working with single people, and the progress I was having organizing singles events at our church. They interviewed single people from several Lutheran churches around the country for the article.

One thing I said in my interview was something my youngest daughter said once, "Why do we always have people to our house, and no one invites us to their house."

I told her, "That was just the way it is."

Not many people wanted to do the cooking and cleaning and the work required for entertaining. I found this was one way I could keep my children involved with my church. My Pastor and his wife always came to my dinners and birthday parties for my children, so I knew others I invited would be there if he accepted my invitation. I will always be grateful to him for the time he was able to give to me, especially during my divorce, when my nephew died, and then when my sister died. I don't know how people make it who do not have a spiritual community to help them through tough times. When he retired, Brit said, "When is the grandpa pastor coming back? I want the grandpa pastor."

When I read the article from the *Lutheran Brotherhood Magazine*, and what I said in the interview, I thought everyone at church was going to be angry at me. It made our church look insensitive to single people.

The new pastor's wife said to me, "I am going to have you and your children over for a get together."

She meant well, but never did come through with the offer.

~~~~~~~~~~~

Securities License

I started working for a stock brokerage firm when I was still in high school and always wanted to get my license after I turned twenty-one. When I married I put away those plans. My husband at the time seemed to be jealous of the men I was working with and the fact that most of them had college educations. When I was looking for choices of what to do career-wise I decided to take the securities exam, but before I could take the test I had to find a firm that would sponsor me. I had interviewed with some of the big firms but they were not interested in me. I guess I didn't wow them. I finally got the yellow pages out one day and went through the listings for brokerage firms and called until I finally found someone who would sponsor me. The owner of the firm helped me with my registration and then I started studying. When I took the exam I was overwhelmed, it wasn't anything like the test that was given when I was sixteen. I did not recognize many of the questions. I listened to the others who had taken the test and heard them mention a class for taking the exam. I decided I needed to enroll in a similar class to help me pass the exam. I read an advertisement about classes for individuals studying for the securities exam. The classes were held in the evenings as well as in the daytime, and I knew I needed to enroll in these classes if I was going to pass the exam.

Since there were classes in Oakland as well as San Bruno I could attend classes at either location, and still keep my job until I passed the exam. One evening, I decided to attend the class in San Bruno so I could visit with Brit and Case. It was in the child custody papers that I could see them during the week when it wasn't my weekend to be with them.

I called Greg about visiting with Brit and Case before my class, but he said no and hung up on me.

He didn't know I was just around the corner. I debated about going over to talk to him, but decided against that. This might be another of those times when we would get into an argument, and it could develop into something physical. We had one of those times when I went to pick the kids up at his place and I made a remark referring to a problem he had when we were married. He came at me and knocked me down. His wife kept calling his name to stop. I know our children were upset. I should have stopped at the police station on my way home, but didn't want to put Brit and Case through that. He probably would have lost his job over the attack. After he was promoted and wanted to take Brit and Case back east, I was sorry I didn't follow through with the report.

There were ten classes for the securities exam and I took their practice exams until I felt confident I could pass. I was still having problems with the options and margins questions and finally decided to enroll in another class for eight hours for five days and then study for five days in order to take the exam. One Saturday after my class Greg was to bring Brit and Case to San Francisco and we were going to take BART to Walnut Creek. I remember waiting and waiting and waiting for him. He was always late when it was his time to drop them off or pick them up. No matter what time we agreed on, I could never depend on him.

~~~~~~~~~~

Jason

Jason invited me to come over to study at his house for the week. I debated if I should go or not since I needed quiet with no distractions. If we had any problems I knew this would affect my taking the test. I felt it would be better to get away from my house so I wouldn't be distracted by the many things I needed to do. His daughter was living with him, but she was away. We had the house to ourselves and he promised not to distract me. I told him what times I needed to study and when I would take a break. The day before I was to take the exam on Saturday, his other daughter dropped by the house, using her key to let herself in. We were making the bed, and I made a comment about how it was a good thing she hadn't come a few minutes earlier or she would have found us in bed. The wall went up after that comment. I don't know if he didn't hear me correctly or misinterpreted my comment. We went to a movie and still the wall was there. His other daughter returned and had a friend over in the evening. I was ready to go back to Walnut Creek. I stayed the night, but couldn't sleep. I kept waking up and looking at the clock. When I finally did get up I wanted to go into San

Francisco by myself. Jason wanted to drive me in and have breakfast.

I said, "No, I need some time by myself."

I took the test and went back to Walnut Creek. He drove out later and we were going to go out to dinner to celebrate. Our celebration was not much fun. It was very tense. He said he hadn't gone to the bank and borrowed twenty dollars from me to help pay for the dinner. When we got back to my house, we got into an argument, he blamed me for the wall, and then left. I didn't talk to him for some time. At one time we were going to buy a mobile home park together in Washington state that had separate quarters for the owners. I told him we weren't going to live together, so if he was going into this partnership thinking we would then it wasn't going to work out. He would have his separate quarters and I would have mine. Several times he wanted me to move in with him, but I couldn't see that working out with the problems we had with his one daughter.

When Jason's father died his daughter called me to tell me, and to say her dad needed me. I couldn't understand why she was telling me this. When his dad passed away I told Jason I could not stand to go to any more funerals. I had been to my nephew's and my sister's and I couldn't go to anymore except my own. I called his mother before I went to pick up my children and wanted to bring some flowers to her. His brother said they were busy and wouldn't be available, and Jason wasn't there. I guess he was hurt that I would not make it to the funeral. The following weekend he came to my house to hang some shades for me. We talked, had a barbeque and a nice visit, then I sent him home. I told him before that if we were not going to have an exclusive relationship I didn't want him to spend the night anymore. I felt this was not a good example for my children. When July 4th weekend came I decided to go to San Diego. Jason said he was going to be with his mother and would be busy also. I had taken BART to the city and then taken the bus to the airport to save on the cost of parking at the airport. I thought about asking him for a ride, but decided I would make it on my own. When I arrived at the airport I was waiting for my plane when I saw him come into the waiting area. I thought he was bringing one of his daughters to the airport, but when he got closer I could see it wasn't his daughter with him. I didn't know who she was. I waited until they walked past me and thought he would be dropping her off and coming back. When he didn't return I walked down to the runway and looked for him, but he was not there. He had gotten on one of the planes with her. They took a trip together for the 4th, and he was not with his mother. I went to San Diego and stayed with a friend of my roommate. She stayed at my house when she was in the Bay Area and invited me to come to San Diego sometimes to relax and visit. I rented a car because she was out in the suburbs and I would not be able to get around otherwise. She had horses and enjoyed horseback riding every day she could. I hadn't done any horseback riding since I lived in Maryland, when my sisters and I went horseback riding. She wanted to stay out for hours, but after more than an hour my legs and bottom were killing me and it was extremely hot and dusty. She lived in a great place to have horses. All of her neighbors had horses in their backyards. It was horse country.

The following weekend, Jason came to my house to help me install tile for the bathroom floor in the master bedroom. While we were working I asked him what he did 4th of July weekend. He was vague, not giving much information. I let him go on for a while seeing what he would say, just digging his hole deeper and deeper.

Finally, I said to him, "I saw you at the airport. I can tell you what you were wearing. I can tell you what she was wearing and what she looked like."

He smiled and said, "I bet you can tell me what we talked about also."

I told him, "I didn't know you were seeing someone else while we were together." He said, "I started seeing her whenever we were not together and I could talk to her about you."

She became a buddy to him and when his father died she was there and I wasn't. I didn't see him anymore for awhile after that. I told him he couldn't spend the night except to sleep on the couch.

Sometime later I won a trip to Carmel as a financial planner and since the trip was for two I asked Jason. I wasn't sure how it would work out, but usually we only had problems when we were around his daughter. The weekend was great and when we were driving back we were discussing our future together. The holidays were coming up and this would be a test. He called me later and said his daughter already arranged Thanksgiving with her mother and he would be having Thanksgiving with them. We had plans to go to my office Christmas party together, but he called me a few days before the party and said he couldn't go.

I told him, "No problem, I will invite someone else."

He was surprised that I would be able to do that on such short notice.

When Case was about four and we were outside saying our good-byes to Jason, when Case told him "I want a dad at my mom's house." We both laughed at this little guy speaking his mind. What a great compliment. He was trying to get a dad for our family. He never said that to anyone else.

<hr />

Day Camp: *1987*

I saw an ad in the local paper for day camp in our neighborhood, but the age limit was six years old. I wanted to enroll Brit and Case, and thought about saying Case was six and not five.

Brit said, "Well, if he is going to be six then I am going to be nine."

I didn't think it was such a good idea to encourage my children to lie, and for me to make excuses that it was okay in my circumstance, so I gave up on that idea, and we waited another year. The day camp was a life saver for all of us. They enjoyed the camaraderie of the other children, the crafts and the outings they took each week. The most important thing was they met another camper who lived in our neighborhood. They were of similar ages and in the evening, they always wanted to go up to see their friend and his dad. They had a pool and the dad would cook them dinner. I was so glad to see they were having a good time and were so happy. I wanted to meet both of them, so I invited them to a barbeque at our house. I found out that he and his wife had divorced, but she had custody of their son. Every summer all three of them looked forward to day camp, and even talked about becoming camp counselors when they were fourteen. After that when they were with me all three were at our house or their friend's house. Eventually their friend's dad sold the house and moved to an apartment, but asked if he could use my address so his son could go to school in the Walnut Creek district.

The dad took them camping one weekend, and when they returned he told me he had a problem with Case. I thought it was his bed wetting, but he said Case got into a fight with his son.

It really made me sad. I know he was somewhat aggressive when he felt he was being picked on, but his friend was such a gentle person. I could never imagine what had made him turn on him like that. The dad and his son were both very forgiving, and didn't let this ruin their friendship. I never heard of something like that happening again.

~~~~~~~~~~~

Brit and Case Moving to Washington, DC: *1989*

In March I was scheduled to travel to Minneapolis for two weeks of training. Before I left, Case told me their dad was taking a job in Washington, DC and they were moving there with him.

I said, "No, No, you are not moving. You are not going to Washington, DC." While I was in Minneapolis I thought about it and decided if they wanted to go I would let them go. When I returned and told them if they wanted to move I wouldn't fight the issue. Since I was born in Washington and grew up there, I felt the experience would be good for them. I thought they would probably attend one school term and be back like their day camp friend. It was then they both said they didn't want to go. I think they were caught up in the moment, and in the two weeks I was gone they changed their mind. I knew then that I needed to find an attorney to represent me this time and started making calls to find someone I had confidence in. I ended up going to an attorney who was in the same office as my divorce attorney. Greg and I had to be evaluated by a private family counselor and each of us were to be responsible for our own expenses. The counselor also had to come out and interview my roommates and look at the home they would be living in while with me.

After the divorce I felt that Brit and Case were having problems they wouldn't talk about with either their dad or I, and decided to find a counselor to work with them. I felt this would help them relieve some of the stress they might be experiencing due to our divorce. I took them to a counseling school at JFK as the fees would not be as high as with other counselors. Since I could only take them every other weekend when they were with me, most counselors would not work with our schedule. I later found out the counselor who worked on our child custody case was employed at this school. I believe she knew of my case before she met me, but she did not dis-qualify herself from the case.

Case had a friend whose mother and father were

divorcing and the dad would not let his son see his mother.

Case told him, "You should go to counseling like we are and then maybe your dad would let you see your mother."

I thought what an insightful little guy he was. Unfortunately, my taking them to counseling was not something the counselor or court looked on as positive. The interpretation was that I took them to counseling because I was experiencing problems raising them.

While we were going through this custody battle Greg also wanted me to pay him child support when he had them. I had asked for a raise of ten percent and I guess he decided I should be paying him since I had roommates and had extra income. My salary at that time was probably a third of what he made. When I received the court papers asking for me to pay child support, I gave my supervisor my resignation. I had made up my mind there was no way I was going pay this man child support. He left me when I had a six-week-old baby and a two-year-old, with no job, no family, and no friends, and now he wanted me to pay child support. My attorney was not happy with my decision, he thought it was not a good decision to make. I told him this was my statement to the court. I did not intend to pay him child support now or ever. I even thought about kidnapping my children and leaving the country, but I knew this would not be good for them or me, and I would probably end up in jail. All I wanted was a life with them without any battles with their dad. I thought if we could have time to ourselves without conflict from the divorce it would help them find peace and joy. My attorney recommended counseling for me while I was going through this battle so I didn't self-destruct. My boss allowed me to take back my resignation. I think he knew I was going through a difficult time. There was no privacy at work for phone calls, so I am sure most of my colleagues could hear what was going on. I checked with my insurance and they offered ten sessions for counseling, and had a group session for females when I joined.

In the end, the court decided to allow them to move to Washington, DC with their dad. The female counselor thought because of my job as a financial planner I was going to have to work evenings. As it was I eventually went to work for a bank, so my hours were 9–5. In her report she wrote my taking them to counseling was an indication I was having problems dealing with them. Another thing counted against me was that I had roommates. I told Brit and Case one day they were probably going to have roommates and this was a good learning experience for them. Because of my unique life with roommates and my choice of employment the court thought it would be better for my children to move 3,000 miles away. This meant our time together would be limited over their lives. Phone calls and letters can't fill that space. Did they suffer because of this? Is there a hole in their hearts from being away from me over the years? Only they can answer that question. Maybe someday they will write their own book.

Brit was not happy with the decision, and said she didn't want to move. I told her I could go back to court, but if I did she would have to testify.

When I asked her if she would be able to do that, she said no so I didn't pursue the matter.

It was sad to have summer end, and they would be going back to live with their dad for the school year. I always felt their separation anxiety building up to that time. It usually culminated in our having a disagreement over some trivial thing.

One evening before the end of summer I invited their day camp friend and his dad over for a barbeque. It was their friend's birthday, so I made a cake for him. I didn't plan on serving wine, as I wanted Brit and Case to learn that we could celebrate without alcohol at events. It seemed like their friend's dad and I were on the same page because he came to the dinner with a bottle of non-alcohol wine.

Their friend's dad asked me why I went to court in Contra Costa County for child custody, and asked if I knew they usually favored men who went for custody. I told him I didn't know that when we started the proceedings. I didn't know it until he told me, but it was something I felt when I was going through the process. He said that was why his son's mother had gone through the courts in San Francisco, because she knew their courts leaned in favor of the mother for custody. Even though she won custody of her son, he missed his dad so much that as soon as he arrived back east with his mother he was on the phone to his dad. He couldn't talk because he was crying so much. His mother finally realized how much her son missed his dad, and so she gave up custody and he came back to live with his dad. I thought she was a very caring mother to do that, and her son was lucky she put his happiness ahead of hers.

They used my address so he could go to school in Walnut Creek and would come by to pick up mail from the school when necessary. He was always available for my projects around the house, and the money came in handy for extra activities. He was a good worker and I was lucky to have his help. There were not many teenagers who wanted to work in our neighborhood, as their parents were able to give them money whenever they had a need or want.

I decided I was not going to let the court's decision destroy me. There were other children out there that needed my attention and love, so I decided to apply to become a foster parent. I started the process with the fingerprints and background investigations for myself and my roommates. Br and L were living with me at the time and said they didn't have any problem doing the fingerprints, but Cl said he resented the intrusion into his privacy. He did fill out the information, but left shortly after that. I appreciated his helping me paint the inside of my house before he left. He said he didn't expect any payment, but was doing it just to help me out. It would have been impossible for me to paint the stairway and the fifteen-foot high wall in the living room without his equipment and expertise. The next time I painted I only went up to as far as I could get on the ladder and the long handle on the roller would allow, and no one but me could tell the difference where I had left off.

After they moved, Greg called me and said Case needed to talk to me, and he put him on the phone. He was having a hard time adjusting to the move. He didn't think Case would miss me so much, he thought it was going to be Brit that was going to have more problems adjusting. I called weekly and wrote letters. I bought a tape recorder and recording my voice reading *Clan of the*

Cave Bears. I hoped this would help them to stay close to me. Many times, I called to talk to them, but was told they were in bed. I found it strange that the son of his wife was still up, but my children were in bed. Greg traveled nine months out of the year when we were married, so I knew he was not home a great deal. I left messages, but was not sure if they were relayed. It was not always easy getting through to them by phone. I went back to Washington, DC to visit them so I could show them Ocean City, where my older children and I went when they were children. We visited with my friend Jo at her home and made the usual trip to the museums. On another visit I took them to Virginia where my mother was raised. My uncle and aunt had torn down my grandmother's house and built a brick rambler. They originally wanted to restore the house since it was one of the oldest in that community, but because of the costs they decided it made more sense financially to start new. There was talk of the state or county buying the home as a show place of how people lived during the one hundred years the house was there. I don't know what happened to that possibility, but it would have been great for our family members for generations to come back to see how our ancestors lived.

While we were in Virginia one of our distant relatives opened a beauty parlor in her home. Her dad was a carpenter and did all the work, and her shop looked very professional. Brit wanted to have her hair permed, so it would be easier to fix in the morning before going to school. Many times, she asked me to fix her hair before we left on Monday mornings since she didn't have anyone to help her. While Brit was getting her hair done Case and I went looking for Indian arrowheads. We went to an old house that was empty and falling down. It looked like it would be a great place to start. I told him we needed to dig deep into the ground to find arrowheads. Most people in the area found them after digging up ground due to new construction or putting in a garden. We weren't able to find any arrowheads but went back to pick up Brit, and she was very pleased with the outcome. It was nice to see her smiling, as there seemed to be so little of that at times. Afterwards, they were able to take turns riding my cousin's horse, which was a real treat for them.

American Association of University Women: *July 1989*

I had seen a calendar of events for American Associated University Women (AAUW) from a co-worker in San Francisco. The events they had scheduled were of great interest to me. My co-worker told me there was a branch in Walnut Creek, and they had an open house event scheduled. The day of the open house was when Brit and Case were leaving to go back with their dad to Washington. I decided to leave them with Br for the last half-hour before their dad came to pick them up. This would be easier on all of us than waiting for the last minute to say goodbye. Brit was studying me very intently. I think she was waiting for me to start crying as we were hugging and saying goodbye. Luckily, I was able to contain myself until I got out to the car.

It was a good thing I had something to take my mind

off their leaving, and joining AAUW helped me to fill a small spot of the void in my life.

I joined their board of directors and the first project I accepted was a fundraiser for scholarships. I read a book that I thought would make a good workshop for women and girls in the area. The last name of one of the authors was the same as someone I worked with. I asked him if they were related, and he said she was his mother, and the co-author lived in the area. I went through the telephone book and started calling anyone with her last name. I left messages at each location and received a return call from her. When she returned my call, I asked if she would be interested in giving her seminar for our fundraiser and she responded she would. The workshop seminar was held at my church in Walnut Creek, which didn't charge us for use of the space. The fundraiser was the most successful they had ever experienced.

She remained in touch after the event, and invited me to join her Friday morning women's prayer group. It was a nice group and we continued this group for some months. After she and her husband sold their house she moved to San Francisco, and we lost contact.

The next office I held was as president. My good friend Mary was the current president and I worked with her during her year to see what my duties would entail. It was sometimes difficult filling the officer spaces, everyone was busy. Since I believed in their mission to help other women continue their college education it was hard to say no. I read as much as I could on leadership and worked to keep the group on track when we had board meetings. They were a great bunch of women and I was lucky to have so much help during my term as president.

~~~~~~~~

My New Kitchen

I decided to give myself a new kitchen for a birthday present. The kitchen had not been remodeled since it was built, so the flooring was the original avocado green linoleum. The counter tile was outdated and the sink needed to be replaced. I usually gave myself a trip for my birthday, but this year I decided to have the updates completed so I could enjoy my new kitchen before I sold the house. I met a contractor in the paint store and asked him if he would come by and give me a bid on the work I was contemplating. His price was quite reasonable, in fact I think he might have underbid the job. It took him a week of work from early in the morning until evening to complete the small job. I asked Br not to do any deep-frying during the daytime while he was working in the kitchen. He put up sheets separating the kitchen from the family room so the dust from the work wouldn't get in the family room and the living room. One morning before I left for work, Br was in the kitchen making donuts. I had to ask her again not to cook except what was really necessary in the morning, and she could cook after he left. She told me the contractor liked her donuts and she was making them for him. She got up early before he came and made donuts for him the rest of the week. I am sure she spent a lot of time talking to him, so maybe that is why it took so long to finish the job. I believe she probably shared with him my comment that, "I was getting the work done for such a good price," and he knew he might have under-bid this job.

I joined the gourmet dinner group with the American Association of University Women, and it was my turn to have the monthly dinner at my house. I looked forward to these evenings with such pleasant people. Sometimes I had a date and other times I took one of the other ladies from AAUW who was available. My sink and dishwasher were laying out in the yard to be reinstalled after the tile was finished. I made the decision I had to use paper plates, or cancel the event. We all looked forward to the tables set with the good china, glassware, silver, candles and real flowers. If paper plates were used it should be extenuating circumstances. I knew once the group saw my kitchen they would understand. My friend Bn came over to help me make the curry dish, which was his specialty, along with the curried prawn soup.

He said, "Doesn't it bother you that you have twenty people coming for dinner and your kitchen is a mess?"

I told him, "There is nothing I can do about that, except close the door from the kitchen to the dining room."

Most of the people coming to the dinner had gone through some remodeling of their house, so they knew what I was going through. The contractor told me it would be finished before my dinner and I was already committed to the dinner. The kitchen was just a minor inconvenience. It turned out most of the kitchen was back in shape so it didn't look as bad at 7:00 p.m. as it had looked at 5:00 p.m.

CHAPTER SIXTEEN

~~~~~~~

L

When L moved in Ma had another mother to guide her. L's mother died when she was younger. I am not sure if her losing her mother at an early age had left a big hole in her heart, but I think she thought I was going to be able to fill that space. I took her to the singles group so she could get acquainted with other singles her age. She graduated from college to be a teacher and then decided she didn't like teaching so she joined the Navy and went back to school for her master's degree. She moved to the Bay Area to go to school for court reporting and worked while taking classes. She was a great help around the house when we had our big house cleaning events twice a year. The first Thanksgiving she was living at my house she invited her friends to join my family for dinner. She did her cooking late at night but did not clean up behind herself, so when I got up at 5:30 a.m. to put my turkey in the oven I had to clean up before I could get started. After dinner she left with her friends and left me and Bett with the dishes to wash. Br and Ma always went to her mother's for holidays so she was not home. When L came home I was still angry about her mess in the kitchen from cooking, then leaving without helping with the dishes. I told her if she wanted to invite friends she had to do her share of the cleaning afterwards. A few months later her dad and his wife came out to stay for a short visit, and she gave them her bedroom. When I went downstairs I didn't see her sleeping on the couch. I couldn't figure out where she was sleeping, until she popped out from behind the couch. She decided to sleep on the floor behind the couch which gave her more privacy. I really didn't like to encourage family and friends for overnight guests, but since this was for a short visit it wasn't going to be a problem. They usually went out for dinner since they wanted to see all the sights around San Francisco and Napa. Her family invited me out to dinner with them a couple of times. They said they were appreciative to me for opening my home to L and helping her to adjust. Bett started a new job at a restaurant in the city and invited me to dinner where she was working as a waitress. I took L along to be my designated driver in case I had an extra glass of wine. Bett seemed to be upset about the change of plans. She referred to L as "my other daughter." Maybe there was sibling rivalry going on, it's hard to understand. I didn't think it would be a problem, but I guess it was with Bett.

One morning she and a male roommate were in the bathroom getting ready for work. I heard "*****" and "******" and then some shoving and more shouting. L said they shared the bathroom before and never had any problems, since there were two sinks and the toilet area were separated by a door. Both of them needed to leave at about the same time and usually worked around one another brushing their teeth, combing their hair and last minute details. I believe the incident in the bathroom may have been due to the fact that both of them were single and close in age, and L rejected his wanting to be romantically involved.

I was going through some difficult times myself. I had a high-pressure job selling financial products and meeting my weekly quotas. I also had problems with Bett and didn't want to share what was going on with her. They both thought my moods were due to my love life. L thought whenever I was having any problems I took my frustration out on them. My mother had a stroke and I was concerned she was not going to make a full recovery. There was also the custody battle, and she and Br had been interviewed by the counselor. I never asked them what they said in their interview. There wasn't any good in going over that now. L decided to move and was going to find roommates who would share a house with her. Br was going to move with her, but the only problem with their arrangement was when they lost a roommate they each would have to make up the difference. Whereas, in my home I didn't change the rent when someone moved out, it always stayed the same, so this made the move unaffordable for Br, otherwise I am sure she would have moved. L lived with me for over four years. I thought we had a good relationship while we lived together, but she never came back to see me. I saw her in downtown Walnut Creek and she avoided me. I guess all relationships are tested.

Tm, a Male Roommate

I met Tm at one of the singles events. He had been dating someone for some time but felt like he was being used for the dinners and other events he would pay for while dating. He was looking for a place that was not as expensive so he could pay off some of his debt. I told him I had a room available and what the price was so he came to take a look and liked what he saw. It was just going to be temporary for him, but he ended up staying for almost four years. He stayed until he and L had a big blow-up in the bathroom. He had a habit of giving me checks that didn't have sufficient cash in the account. One time I went to the bank, and I had a feeling someone's check was not going to clear. I don't know why I had that premonition, that was the first time. I usually kept extra funds in my account because of that. Later when he came home he gave me a check for twenty-five dollars because he knew the check was going to be refused for insufficient funds. He did that several times, and I let it pass. I knew he would give me a check for twenty-five dollars to cover the costs and the check would clear.

San Francisco Earthquake: *October 1989*

The earthquake was a wake up for how vulnerable we all were. I had an appointment scheduled that day that would have taken me to Oakland. The couple I was meeting with decided to hold off until a better time, and we agreed to meet later. That cancellation might have saved my life when I saw how the overpass went down and people below were killed. There was no way to get gas or food since the electricity was out all over the Bay Area. There was only one thing to do, go home. That was the only time all of the roommates were together. L picked up a movie that we all watched and after the movie the cable came on and we saw what disasters had taken place all over the area. I thought of starting a photo business in the Ghirardelli area which is a big tourist area, but was doing my research to consider my choices. It was a good thing I hadn't started the business, because people could not get into work in the city due to the Bay Bridge collapse and the freeway repairs which would take sometime. I would have lost my house if I had not been able to make the lease payments for my business. A good thing I was taking my time and not rushing into anything.

~~~~~~~~~

Zephyr Cove

I visited Zephyr Cove with the singles group and when I received their calendar for a family Christmas event, my son FJ and I decided to give it a try. The family enjoyed going to Tahoe for Christmas, and Bett and FJ liked to go skiing when we were there. Several times we rented a condo, but at the Zephyr Cove Presbyterian Christmas event we didn't have to buy food, do the cooking, or the cleaning up. It was all done for us just like Lake Sequoia. The event started on December 26th and for four days they did the cooking and all we had to do was make a bag lunch each day for going out and enjoying the snow.

One year we rented a cabin at Zephyr Cove from a pastor for December 24th and 25th, and then went to the family event afterwards. Since the pastor had to give the message for Christmas Eve and Christmas Day at his church he wasn't able to use his cabin. That time Bett, FJ, their dad, my grandson, as well as Brit and Case, and my roommate L rented the cabin. It was glorious to wake up on Christmas morning on the beautiful lake. We had a marvelous time and went into Tahoe to have dinner at one of the casinos. This became a regular event at Zephyr Cove at Christmas time for all of us. Brit and Case usually shared a room with me with bunk beds for all. In the evening there was a wonderful dinner, then there was a family worship time with crafts and game playing until bedtime. People had a hard time understanding why my former husband was along on the trip. They had never seen this work for the many divorced couples they knew. I think the reason it worked was that neither of us were married. Brit, Case and I went to Zephyr Cove one summer with the singles group, but children were required to sleep downstairs and the adults were in rooms on the second floor. I tried to tell the organizer that we usually came here in the winter and they always stayed with me and didn't want to sleep with people they didn't know. There was no changing the leader's mind as this was the way they had always done the event, and so we didn't stay for the weekend even though I already paid and wouldn't receive any funds back.

At one time, my son FJ and I thought about buying

a condo in the area, but after driving back in bumper to bumper traffic with the requirement to put on snow chains, we changed our minds. My drive was only four hours, but his drive was nine hours to Southern California.

~~~~~~~~~

Nu

Nu was a Japanese student attending classes at Berkeley. She wanted to rent the master suite so she could have a private bathroom. At first it was difficult to give up my big room and move into one of the smaller rooms. Once I got used to it and looked at the big picture, I was able to handle the choice. If I wanted to stay in my house until I decided to sell, I needed to increase my income to cover my expenses with the house. She was a very clean, quiet person, but we had a difficult time communicating with her because her English wasn't very good. She cooked for herself in the evening and one time bought all the ingredients for sushi and taught us how to make it ourselves. I thought this would be a great experience for Britt, Case, and Ma, but they didn't seem to be interested. Whatever was on television was more interesting. We said we were going to try to learn some Japanese while she stayed, but it wasn't an easy language to learn. She was very patient with us, and invited us to come to Japan to see her when she moved back to be with her family. One time we were having problems with mice in the wintertime. They usually came in looking for a warm place and food. They found a way to get in the house under the pantry. They mainly destroyed the cereal and sugar. After we had cleaned out the pantry and I filled in their entrance with poison there usually was no longer a problem. Nu threw away every item on her shelf, even the canned goods, because the mice might have had contact with the container. She was very concerned about germs and even wore a face mask and gloves while throwing away her pantry items.

Bett Remarries: *1993*

Bett moved to Southern California after her marriage ended, and had been renting a room from another female. It was a nice condo and she had a job selling jewelry at one of the large department stores. Things were working out for her after the move from the Bay Area. Her brother and dad lived close by so she had family support if it was needed. She called me and told me she had met someone and they were getting married after a whirlwind few weeks. She couldn't be talked out of rushing into this marriage. Her dad and brother were not supportive of the event and were not planning on attending. I was ready to rush down to help them celebrate and had been shopping for a negligee for her wedding gift. Her roommate decided she needed the room for family, and so she was out of a place to live and moved in with her brother for a short while. She was married shortly after that, and became pregnant immediately. She wanted to have children for some time, as her biological clock had been ticking. They bought an ice cream parlor, and it looked like things would work out, but then she had to take over running the business. It was not easy on her, I know, because she was on her feet a great deal of the time. When the shop closed in the evening she had to clean up and mop the floors. Brit, Case and I went down to visit her when she first opened and we had a celebration. She hired some of the local young people in the area occasionally, but I am sure the profits walked out the door with the friends and family discounts as soon as she was gone. After several months away, her husband came back to help with the business and await the birth of their first child. It wasn't long after his return that Bett came back to the Bay Area to live with me. They couldn't both run the business together and have two bosses. She didn't like the way he treated her and talked to her in a condescending way. She has always been very sensitive when she felt someone was talking down to her. I tried to make sure when I said anything to her that I kept my voice and tone down. While she was with me she had offers from men who wanted to take her out on a date.

I told her, "No, you are a married woman, and you are pregnant. If you want to go out I will take you to a movie and we can go out for dinner as long as I have a coupon for the restaurant."

When her daughter was born her husband drove up to Walnut Creek for the birth and made it before she was delivered. Bett was hooked up to a monitor and was very uncomfortable. I think she was surprised at how painful childbirth can be, since I never said anything about pain during my deliveries. We both went into the delivery room. When the baby was born the umbilical cord was wrapped around her neck, and her color was grayish.

Bett kept asking "Why isn't she crying, what's wrong?"

Her husband and I were both standing during the delivery as there were no chairs. We watched the nurse as she worked on the baby and she kept looking up at the clock. The nurse had been trying to reach the doctor, but he hadn't shown up. Finally, after several minutes which seemed like forever, the baby cried, and we were so relieved. I couldn't stand up another second. I was afraid we were going to witness the birth and death all at one time. Now I understand why hospitals don't like to have family in the delivery rooms. It is wonderful as long as everything goes OK, but when it doesn't people can panic and become hysterical. Luckily, I am not a hysterical person and was able to remain calm.

It was a good thing that I had a room available and the rent was something that would be affordable for her. Friends from church had given her baby items, as well as my roommates, and a neighbor gave away her baby items since she did not plan on having any more children. Staying home with her daughter and taking care of her needs was all that she wanted to do. She applied for AFDC since she wasn't receiving any support from the dad. A big plus was since she had the companionship of my other roommates she didn't experience the baby blues after the birth. Everyone wanted to hold the baby and take care of her. We took a drive to Napa and did some wine sipping since I had to drive and did not want to drink. Afterwards we went to a local restaurant and had a cappuccino and split a dessert. I spent less than five dollars for the day. I wanted her to see that she could have a good time without spending a great deal of money.

I asked her if she would like to have the baby baptized on Christmas Day since all of the family would be together. I talked to our pastor and he met with both parents and we had special day for her baptismal and Christmas. I bought her a christening dress with the eighty-five dollars of lotto money I won, but when I came home they had already purchased one. After several months, she and her husband started talking about going away for the weekend. They were talking about moving back to Fresno again. He had sold the ice cream parlor and was looking at other business opportunities.

<hr>

Ka Moves In: *October 1994*

While Bett was living with me I had a new roommate move in. I rented her my master suite with a private bathroom for the additional income. It wasn't easy to move into the smaller room again, but after I made the move it seemed quite cozy. I was sharing a bathroom now with the other roommates which was not a big problem because I took my bath in the evening and could put on my makeup in the bedroom if needed. After Ka moved in I realized there was going to be a problem with her son who was not employed and had no place to live. She also had a daughter who cleaned rooms at a local motel who was pregnant by her boyfriend. Bett was going back with her husband and would be moving. I decided that I wanted to get away from roommates and the problems it entailed. I gave Ka notice to move and then she became very vindictive. I invited her and her family to spend

Thanksgiving with us, but she turned down the offer. My son and grandson had driven up from Southern California so we had a full house.

After Thanksgiving Day, I again invited her to join us for leftovers, but she said no.

We had just finished eating and I was cleaning up. Ka came down to the kitchen to get her package of frozen peas that she used for her back. She made a remark to Bett regarding some personal information she shared with Ka. Bett took off after her with her husband and my son FJ, right behind her to stop her. Ka's daughter came out of her mother's room, and Bett and her took a couple of swings at each other. At this time Bett was several months pregnant. We got them separated and had just settled down when the police showed up at my door. Ka had called them saying she had been attacked. The police made her daughter leave since she was part of the problem. From then on, Ka was constantly calling the police for every minor problem. She was also letting her son stay in her room. I had to go to court and have a restraining order against her two children. After going to court I agreed that her son and daughter could help her move for a couple of hours a day when Bett would be out of the house. As it was, the court order was changed by the judge and she was given more time than I agreed to, but by then there was nothing I could do. When Bett came home in the evening Ka's daughter was to be out of the house. Several times Ka called the police saying that Bett was not supposed to be there per the court agreement. Later when I read the police report I was greatly surprised at what had been written by the police officers of the incidents and how they had not been written up correctly. I finally had to go to an attorney and have her served with an eviction notice to protect myself. It was at that time that an agency that did credit reports for landlords called me and said I could have avoided having this type of tenant if I had used their service. They told me she had previously been evicted from other residences, but didn't share what the reason was.

It was a very stressful thirty days until she moved. Brit, Case and FJ would be with me for Christmas and Ka was to be out by New Year's Eve. Brit and I were going to be ushers at the Nutcracker Suite in Oakland and Case didn't want to join us. I thought this would be something we could do as a family together that we both enjoyed. Brit did a great job ushering and we did have a nice time. I just wished Case wanted to participate, but he wanted to stay in Walnut Creek. I don't think he realized how long it was going to take and I worried about leaving him alone. When we drove around the corner I saw him outside looking for my car. I think he was very relieved to see us. I felt bad about leaving him. I knew Ka was a very disturbed person. She would constantly turn the water on in the bathroom, leave the house and let it run continually. If we saw her leave and the water was running upstairs we had to turn off the water for the entire house. She also kept her windows open when she went out of the house, so I had to turn the heat back when she was gone. This resulted in her putting in another call to the police saying we were preventing her from using the water. I think she liked the attention, even though it was very negative attention. I also had to give notice to

Br to move at this time since she and Ka seemed to have become friends. My attorney said when Ka moved if she came back to visit Br there was nothing I could do. Br's brother came from back east to help her find an apartment and move. Ka told him how afraid she was of us and asked if he would stay around until they finished moving. He didn't realize what a great help he had been to us by being there. She seemed to almost act like a normal sane person when he was around, which must have been really difficult for her. I think she may have been trying to play the helpless female part with him as her knight in shining armor to her rescue.

I kept telling myself this would be over soon, we would have a life again and we didn't have to act like animals during this difficult time. When she was finally out of the house it was a great relief and we could finally celebrate. I was very generous with Br when I returned her deposit, giving her extra interest on her funds. I was grateful for all the help, but was sorry it was ending like this. She had lived in my house for over seven years.

Bett Moves Out on My Birthday: *1995*

Bett and her husband stayed with me until the end of January. I came home from work and she had moved out without even telling me her plans. It came as a great shock. I had been out to dinner with a friend as it was my birthday, and was greatly surprised to see what a mess they left. It was a difficult evening. My friend had never seen me this upset and felt bad about leaving me alone. I don't know why they did this to me after I helped them during their many difficult times. I received a call regarding some financial problems her husband had, and after I shared the information with Bett the relationship with her husband deteriorated. He even talked about all of us moving in together to save money on the rent. Why would he want me to move in with them and then move out of my house so suddenly?

They moved and rented an apartment close to where they had the ice cream parlor. Soon after they bought a dog food store business, but it too closed not long after their purchase. Bett decided to get out of the marriage and move because she was pregnant and it would be easier to move with just one child. She found a very inexpensive apartment close to the airport. After her son was born I went to visit and saw that most of the other mothers living there were on AFDC and spent most of their time watching soap operas and sleeping late. People didn't seem to start coming out of their apartments until it was dark and that's when the trouble started. The police were continually called to the apartment complex due to drugs being sold and fights going on between the renters. The couple next door was bringing in their groceries when someone ran in their apartment and as quick as a flash snatched his money belt off the couch. Evidently someone had been watching them and saw the opportunity for quick money. I think Bett went through a "down" period this time after her son was born. She didn't have my roommates and other female companionship to help her through this delivery. She didn't want to go back to work, but I was worried she would end up like these other welfare mothers if she didn't go back to work. I suggested maybe she should try working part-time to see if she could handle working and taking care of two children. Luckily the state was paying for childcare to help mothers get off welfare and back to work. She found good daycare facilities with the state's help and tried out a couple of temporary jobs. By this time, she knew that she liked working and didn't want to stay home worrying about money. She wanted to be able to buy a home and knew that wouldn't happen if she didn't have a good paying job.

She found a townhouse she liked and the owner was selling the units by carrying the mortgage. She asked her father and I to cosign for her. I considered it, but decided it would not be a good idea to get involved in more of her financial matters. As it was, when she decided to move from the townhouse she found that she could not get out of the contract very easily. She tried selling the unit, but since there were several already on the market she gave up and walked away from the property. I am thankful that I didn't cosign because it would have affected my credit rating and made it more difficult for me to refinance or to buy another house later.

After I had my house back again and had some free time to myself I decided I would stay in my house for another year and look for new roommates.

CHAPTER 17

Mi: *1995*

Mi answered my ad and I offered to pick her up and bring her to my house to see the room, as she didn't have a car. She needed a place to stay immediately and was anxious to move. I don't think things were working out where she was. She didn't have much monthly income, but I decided to take a chance on her. When I moved her, she had her belongings all stuffed into large trash bags. She didn't have much to move so we could do it in one load. The rent of three-hundred and fifty dollars per month, which included utilities, was very cheap for the area. I allowed her to use my phone and she paid for her telephone charges. She had a strange habit of keeping her eyes closed when she talked to me. Many times, I wanted to say something but I just tried to overlook it and let it pass. Every morning she would open the door, stand in the doorway, and look out to see what the weather was like. It was like clockwork. She had a hard time keeping a job and I think she was just holding on until she could retire. If she was let go from one job she went out and found another job. Some of her jobs were telemarketing, or sales clerk at the local department stores. She took the bus until she finally was able to buy a car. I thought she was being taken advantage of and she was paying too much money for a car that had over 100,000 miles, but she was adamant it was a good decision. She stayed with me for about a year while waiting to get into an apartment for senior citizens. I know she called regularly to see where she stood on the list and finally her number came up and she was given her own place.

When she left I started to help her load some of her things when she yelled at me, "Leave my things alone. Don't touch them."

I couldn't believe how her behavior changed so drastically. We never had any disagreements, but I wouldn't consider us best friends either. I thought we had a good relationship, but we were just housemates. Sometime later after she moved she went to the store where my friend worked and asked about me. My friend told her that I sold the house and moved. I couldn't understand why she would be inquiring about me after her behavior on her last day at my house.

GI

GI was a young man who worked as a security guard and had goals of becoming a policeman. He was taking classes at the community college that would help him qualify for the position when he applied. The rent was affordable for him, as he had just bought a new car.

His room was directly beside mine and he would get up at 2:00 a.m. to leave for work at 4:00 a.m. He was back and forth from his room to the bathroom. He did his exercises in the morning, and I could hear him lifting his weights and grunting as he did them. Before he left he would go outside and start his car and let it run for fifteen to twenty minutes thinking this was good for the engine. He usually went to bed very early. One evening, at about 8:30 p.m., I was downstairs on the phone as I had just received a telephone call. He came downstairs and tried to take the phone out of my hand. He wanted me to hang up and get off the phone. He said it was disturbing his sleep. I continued my conversation and he kept harassing me to hang up. He was acting like a bully. After this blow-up I could see it was not going to work out for us to be housemates. He wanted me to disconnect my phone when he was sleeping so it would not disturb him. I sympathized with him, but told him that was not going to happen. His request was unrealistic. After this incident his behavior changed and he became very hostile. I told him that it would be best if he found another place to live, and if he continued to cause me stress and grief until he moved out of my house it could affect his rental record if I had to relay any negative information on his stay. If he wanted to join the police force they would do a background check and this negative information could affect his employment and any of his rental prospects in the future. Thankfully he decided to move, and his behavior improved.

Js

Js was a married man whose wife called about the room for him. She was moving out of the area to open a business, and he was staying until he finished his classes at the community college. He also had a job as a security guard. I told him my problem with the previous roommate regarding his schedule and he said that he would be very quiet. When he came home from his job he would take his shoes off and went directly to bed. He kept his word to me. When his wife called and he was not home she asked me if he was seeing someone else. I guess word had gotten back to her about another woman. I told her I hardly saw him because of our schedules. I don't think she believed him because he received divorce papers from her. After that he tried to pursue a relationship with me. I had a hard time understanding his English because of his accent. He helped me plant some new trees in my back yard. I had to have trees removed because of disease and replanted the same type of tree. It was depressing without my trees. I had not seen my neighbors for some years and now I lost my privacy. It would take several years for the trees to get height on them and by then I would probably be gone. He fixed dinner a couple of times and invited me to join him. He was very good looking and a complete gentleman. He had hopes of going back to South America to run for office in his home town, just like Jack Kennedy had done for the senate. I told him the drug dealers would kill him if he crossed them, but that didn't seem to be a concern for him. He wrote poetry to me and gave me several sentimental cards. Our conversations were limited since he could not make himself understood due to his limited English. I had a nightmare one night after watching *Schindler's List* and woke up stifling a scream. I wasn't sure if he heard me, but the next day I explained I had a nightmare. My room didn't have a lock on the door, but he never came into my bedroom. Once I had a nightmare about him coming in, so I guess it was on my mind. He finally decided to move to rejoin his family. I never heard from him after that.

***

Fr

Fr was a widower after twenty years of marriage. His wife had died of cancer. He had quite a bit of furniture and was concerned where he would put all of it since he was moving out of a house he had been in for some time. He came and saw the room and liked my furniture and decided to keep it. He rented two rooms and used one room as a sitting room and the other a reading room. It had always been my goal to have just two roommates to rent two bedrooms each to cut down on the amount of people in the house. For most people that was more than they wished to spend since they didn't spend that much time in their room. Single people are out and about most of the time, so renting one room fits their lifestyle. I allowed Fr to use part of the garage to store some of his furniture, but had him leave me room to put my car in the three-car garage. There was room in front of the house for two cars and two cars in the driveway so none of my roommates would need to park in front of my neighbor's house. Fr was retired so he was at home a great deal. He was dating a few women from the singles group, but I told him about the rule about no overnight guest without my prior approval. I didn't want my house to become his love nest with women in and out of the house at all hours. I was sleeping when I heard some noise at 2:00 a.m. I got out of bed and heard noise coming from his bedroom. My closet wall was the next to his bedroom, and the noise came through the vents also. Evidently, he had a female in his room and they were extremely excited and caught up in the moment. She must have left before morning because I never saw any of the women he dated at my house. It looked like things were going to work out until he started becoming demanding and very bossy. He wanted to be in charge and because of his previous job he was accustomed to being the boss. He was constantly moving his things in the garage and my parking space seemed to get smaller and smaller. I made a retreat area in my yard where I had my lawn chairs and some plants and flowers arranged. When I wasn't outside I enjoyed looking out at the spot I made. It looked so quaint and gave me a feeling of relaxation just by gazing out my kitchen window. Fr decided he wanted to leave my chairs turned upside down so when he went outside he wouldn't have to wipe the chairs off before he sat down. I asked him to please leave my garden areas as I left them since I enjoyed them the way they were. He could bring his own lawn chairs into the yard and make a garden area for himself at a different location. He received an offer from a friend to housesit for a six-month period and decided to take that and possibly buy a house at a later date. He had been renting for the past twenty-five years, so it was going to be difficult to buy in the Bay Area now without a large down payment. I think he was even considering moving back to North Carolina where it was more affordable to buy a house. So, there I was again running an ad for another roommate.

April 1998

Er did not have a car and needed to be close to work since his only mode of transportation was a bike. He was youthful looking and small in stature. I saw him one night as I was returning home on his bike talking to another fellow on a bike. He was very quiet. He rose early in the morning as he had to be at work by 6:30 a.m. He came in about 3:00 p.m. and I never saw him until one morning I had to be at an early meeting and he was fixing his lunch and breakfast. I had to get up at 2:00 a.m. once to let him in because he forgot his key. I could tell he was drinking and was carrying in more beer. He said he was out knocking for half an hour. I told him he was lucky I heard him. The next evening at 2:30 a.m. I heard someone outside and I could see the head of the individual had straight hair so I knew it wasn't Er. I heard someone come in and I leaned over the rail and asked, "What's going on?" He said, "I have a friend with me who is going to spend the night." I said, "Okay" and went to bed. I heard him downstairs and I thought he had fallen. He had been drinking and was warming food in the microwave. I went down and told him he was being very loud. He said he was trying to be quiet. I went back to bed. I heard him again in his room making lots of noise. I finally had to knock on his door and ask him to have his friend leave. They were not going to be able to stay and continue their drinking and noise. He said he would leave also then and move out. I said, "fine, I will give you your money back when you have your things out of the house." He said he wasn't going any place now and slammed the door. I went back to my room and was reading when he came to my door again and wanted to talk. I told him this was not going to work. He was going to have to have his friend leave. He told me that he was entitled to have a friend over to spend the night. He was loud and belligerent and was nose-to-nose with me. He probably felt that because I was a female he could intimidate me. Bn, another roommate, came to the hallway and wanted to know if everything was okay. Er told him he wasn't making any noise and he was entitled to have a friend over. Bn told him that he was noisy and that he heard him slamming the doors and loud conversation. Er went past Bn and shoved him. Bn didn't respond. When he went into his room we could hear his loud conversations about how he was going to go ballistic and hurt someone. When I heard this conversation, I knew it was not going to get any better and decided to call the police. It was not something I wanted to do, but I knew it was not going to get better. I went downstairs and called the police. This was the only time in eighteen years I called the police on a roommate. I was afraid he was going to come down the stairs before I could get them on the line. When they answered the officer stayed on the line until the police arrived at the door. I told the officer the roommate and his friend had been drinking and were continuing to drink and were loud. When the officers arrived, they asked if he had any weapons and I said I didn't know. They went to the room and knocked and Er came to the door. He tried to close the door, but the officers wanted the door open. They asked the other person in the room their name and age. He was a fourteen-year-old boy. If I had turned on the light I would have seen this was a young boy, but hadn't thought about this problem. They asked Er if he had been drinking and he said he had about ten beers. The young boy said he only had a couple of sips. Er was very aggressive with the officers and they finally had to handcuff him and also the young boy. One officer held him down and Er was continuing to be aggressive. When another officer came they took Er out to the car and arrested him for contributing to a minor. They took the young boy to the station and called his father who was going to come and take him home. The female officer said there was something wrong with a thirty-eight-year-old man who was bringing home a fourteen-year-old boy. When Er moved in he said he wouldn't be having anyone over but his son. I put in the lease that he could only have someone over one night in the year. I told him if it was his son we would make an exception. He had a seven-year-old son that he seemed concerned about and was going to send him something for Easter. I told the officers I felt bad for him, he seemed like he was trying to get his life together. I hoped he would be able to keep his job. They said they would probably let him go around noon when he was sober and it would be up to the District Attorney if they would prosecute. After they left I went in his room to turn the light out. He didn't have a bed, just an air mattress, television, a light and his clothes. He had several bags of empty beer cans in his room, and a bottle to Peppermint Schnapps and a bottle of a chocolate alcohol drink. I wiped up the beer that had been spilled and shut the door. I went back to bed to read and had some warm milk in order to get to sleep. I was reading and heard someone outside. I could see it was the police again. I went to the door and the officer had come back for some personal articles, the young boy's coat, gloves and skateboard. He left with the articles and said have a good evening. I went back to bed again to read, but sleep wouldn't come to me.

Before this incident I had a dream that I had evicted Er and when I woke I couldn't understand why I dreamed this. He had been a quiet person, and no problem. Other than the beer cans in the trash he seemed okay. I guess my subconscious was telling me a different message.

After this episode I was driving home one night and a rock flew at my car's front window. It didn't break, but I thought it was intentionally thrown and it might have been Er.

~~~~~~~~~~~~~~~~~~

Bn from Missouri

Bn called long distance from Missouri. He was coming out to California to take a new job and needed a place to stay temporarily. I told him what the rent was and sent him an application telling him that I needed sixteen dollars for the credit check. He sent the application back with a deposit, and I ran the credit check and then sent him the directions to the house. I told him I was sure he would like my home and that after thirty days if he wanted to leave, no problem. He came late on Friday night the week after Easter and I had stopped off with friends after work. Heather let him move in because it was getting dark. I said no problem. We moved a mattress upstairs so he could sleep on that. He figured he would have to sleep on the floor. I said we could move the bed frame up also, but he said he didn't want to get too comfortable because he would be moving as soon as his wife sold the home and the children were out of school. He said he was surprised that a female living alone with other roommates would consider someone they had never seen to move into their house. I told him it was because he was from Missouri, and I felt comfortable after receiving his credit report. He said he would help with the lawn, but didn't like to do housework. He cut the grass for me once and helped me bury some sprinklers that were sticking up. After the incident with Er I told him I was going to sell the house, but probably wouldn't be moving until July or August. He felt that would be about the time he would be leaving also, since his family would be here. He had a cell phone he carried around with him in case his wife called. Their family had an 800 number so it would be inexpensive for him to call and talk. He was quite loud on the phone and I asked if he could make his calls in his room, since there was a phone upstairs. I noticed that his attitude changed after my request, but I couldn't hear my television program when he got on the phone, and his calls were usually lengthy if it was his family. I noticed he had not cut the grass and I needed it cut for the weekend since I was having an open house to start the selling process. The next time I needed to cut the grass I was going away for Mother's Day weekend. I waited to see if he noticed the grass needed cutting, and since he had not mentioned his plan to cut the grass, I decided to do it myself. When I came home from work on Friday, there was a letter from Bn saying he decided to move back to Missouri. The job was not working out and he missed his family. He left his key and a note.

Jm

Jm was an English instructor at the junior college in the area. He was only looking for a short-term arrangement, since he would be teaching for the semester then going back north to his home and teaching there. He had been living with a relative, but decided they would remain friends if he lived elsewhere. He moved in some of his things and then went back home on the weekend to bring his own furniture and bed. He had no problem with me doing a credit check and paid me first and last month's rent. He was a former Berkeley student, as was his wife. He was a quiet, neat person. It was strange at first sitting down and eating together. Then when Bn moved in it became more relaxed as we spent more time together. He agreed to help me with the vacuuming and I could always count on him. He always cleaned up and washed his dishes and put them away immediately. He was very concerned about eating balanced meals, so he spent a good deal of time shopping and cooking his own meals—breakfast and dinner and packing his lunch. Several times when I was home he would come home early and take off for his walk. He always made an effort to get his daily exercise so he wasn't around very much. I felt guilty when I was watching so much television and he would go out and do his jog. He had a strange habit of leaving the cupboard doors open after he was through. I would come into the kitchen and every cupboard door he used would be open. I think this was one of the reasons he didn't live with friends anymore. This was just one of the little things that can bother a person when living with roommates.

BARBARA SHAW

CHAPTER EIGHTEEN

Easter: *1998*

I left on Saturday morning to spend Easter with my family. I attended church in Walnut Creek on Thursday and saw my first Sunday School class taking their first communion. This was the third year I taught the kindergarten Sunday School class. I decided to teach and get more involved or else I probably would have dropped out of going to church. It was hard being single and my children weren't with me every weekend. I usually stayed away from the service on Maundy Thursday because it was hard to see the children with their families together taking their First Communion. It was sad that Brit and Case weren't with me to go through their First Communion.

One of my former pupils, who was only five years old when he was in my class, asked me, "Do you remember me?"

I told him, "Yes, I remember you prayed for a baby brother and a puppy dog, and when your mother told you she was pregnant, you said, 'I know, I prayed for it to happen.'"

He was such a sweet boy, but was still waiting for the puppy dog.

I hoped the students I had would remember the time we had together with good memories. I had Sunday School teachers who were able to encourage me and even came to our home to visit so that my sisters and I would not give up on church.

~~~~~~~

April 1998

I went to see Dr. W, the heart specialist, since my heart was going into atrial fibrillation so often. He said he thought the problem was over. He thought it was just a one-time experience, I told him that it had never stopped completely. I just stopped going into the emergency room because I couldn't stay at the emergency room until after 12 a.m. He said I would have to start on a new medicine otherwise I would probably have a stroke. I had apprehensions about taking any new medications due to past experiences with the side effects. I just didn't want to have a stroke and end up like my mother, paralyzed on one side and in a wheel chair. I would rather visit Dr. Kevorkian.

I think I was partially responsible for my heart problem, because it was the same condition my mother had. When I was going to college and working at the Government Printing Office from 10:00 p.m. until 6:30 a.m. two nights a week, I couldn't stay awake on my first night. Some of the other ladies told me that GPO would let me go if they caught me sleeping at my desk or in the ladies room. She told me they all took diet pills to keep awake. I knew my mother took diet pills to lose weight so I asked her for some of her supply. I took them for two and a half years while I was working on my degree at the community college and then later at University of Maryland. I believe my mother and I had heart problems due to these medications.

~~~~~~~~~~

May 1998

I decided to put the house on the market again. A few people came by, but I received more phone calls this time as I advertised the house as a lease option. I didn't have a for-sale-by-owner sign in front and no open house signs in the neighborhood. I called the neighbor who sold his house, and asked if I could borrow his signs. He gave me some tips on who to call regarding for sale signs and where to obtain a home warranty program for the buyers. He had the same model that I had and I based my listing price on his final selling price.

He was a widower and had been alone for some time. I met him at our community pool. He invited me out to dinner several times, but I was not interested. He invited me to his church for a New Year's Eve party. I said that I was having an open house for friends on New Year's Day, but if I was able to get home early it might be nice. All of my family would be leaving after Christmas and I would be alone and that's when it really was lonely. He said he would pick me up at my house and a friend of his was joining us. We were going to dinner and then to the party. His friend was a female, she was an old friend who was widowed also. They had been engaged over twenty-five years ago, but he came to the US and married someone else, and she went to Canada where she met someone and married. When we arrived at the restaurant he said, "I have something to tell you." You always wonder what is going to come next when someone says those words. He said, "M and I got married yesterday." They had only seen one another for a week after twenty-five years and they were sure this was meant to be. I don't know why he thought he needed to keep his commitment for dinner. He had a good reason for a change of plans.

<center>~~~~~~~~~~~~~</center>

June 2, 1998

I received an anonymous letter from someone saying that I owed them money and if they didn't receive the money they were going to the IRS and would ruin my name by sending out faxes all over the community. Since I was a Certified Financial Planner (CFP) and employed by a bank this person thought he would be able to blackmail me or ruin my reputation. I didn't know who the individual was, but I suspect it was the same individual who had been calling for some time and hanging up. I used the *69 call-back feature one Saturday and no one answered. After I hung up, I received a call every minute from someone saying I had paged them. I had my phone bell off so these calls did not bother me as much as they were intended. I was running an ad for the sale of my house so it did interfere with that since I didn't answer any calls, but just waited for them to leave a message. I called the phone company and they said I had to file a report with the police and receive a case number and then they would put a twenty-four-hour tracer on my telephone line. In that time, I had to keep track of all of the calls when they came in.

After I received the blackmail letter I called the police while I was at work and said I would come by on my way home. When I called in for my messages there was a message from the Walnut Creek Police, they had sent an officer out to my house and then the dispatcher remembered I said I would be coming down to the station. Just what I needed—for the Walnut Creek Police to come to my house again.

I thought the letter and telephone calls might be from one of my previous disgruntled roommates. Since I had to evict one through legal channels and had to ask a few to move, I was sure it was one of them. The more I thought about it I believed it was the person we bought the home from over seventeen years ago. I knew he lived in the neighborhood and his son went to school in the area.

His son came to my door one Halloween when he was out trick-or-treating with some of his friends, and he said, "I used to live here."

I guess L was out in the neighborhood or someone gave him one of my flyers, because he mentioned the sales price of the house. After my experience with the incident with Ka and how things got turned around every time I filed a police report, I lost my confidence in them helping me.

After I filed a complaint and received a case number the telephone company put a tracer on my line. I had to call in every day and report the calls I had received where someone hung up. After two months they finally had a match, but wouldn't tell me who the person was and turned it over to Walnut Creek Police who would call me. I received a message from an officer and called him back. It took about a week of leaving messages for him until I finally talked to him one evening. He asked me about the phone calls and who I knew in Martinez. I told him I wasn't sure. I lived in this house for seventeen years and knew a lot of people all over the Bay Area. I told him about the blackmail letter I received asking for me to turn over my house or my name would be destroyed.

He asked me, "Do you know a person named L?

I told him, "That's the man. I knew it was him. He was the only person who would write this letter and knew the information he did. He also knew I worked for a bank, so he had been following me."

The officer said, "I will be calling L, and will call you after I talk to him."

I stayed up late waiting for the call. It was late when he finally called.

He said, "I have been on the phone the entire time with L, and he denied making the calls and sending the letter. I told him we have it on record."

He said, "L went into the part about the letter, how the escrow had been fraudulent and he wanted to be paid."

I told the officer, "The house was a four-year-old fixer upper when we bought it. There was a huge bleach spot in the family room rug where someone had thrown bleach. The front yard and back yard looked like a jungle. The entire house needed paint, new carpet and new window coverings. He accepted our offer and we returned home thinking we were going to close escrow. His agent called us later and said L wanted more money. We went back and forth with our telephone calls, and I didn't want to give him more money. I said we would buy another house, instead we gave him another $1,000 to complete the transaction. I think he has made some bad financial decisions over the past seventeen years, and now because I am alone he thinks he can intimidate and frighten me into giving him more money."

The officer told him, "If you continue to make these calls you will go to jail."

The officer recommended that I change my phone number.

I told him, "I am selling my home now and even if I did change it, he would probably be able to get the number."

He wasn't convinced that the harassment would quit, and wanted to know if I wanted to file charges.

I told him, "I will think about it."

I didn't sleep well that night and had a hard time at work because I was so tired. After arriving at work, I felt better because of the distraction. There was a man in the bank staring at me and I wondered if he was L.

When I met with the police officer I said, "The letter I have would have L's finger prints on it if they needed that for evidence."

He said, "They don't check for prints except for homicides."

I said, "Oh he has to kill me before they'll check for prints."

He said not to worry, but I knew this guy was mentally unbalanced. He had been holding on to his anger for seventeen years and now he was determined to make it pay off.

I went about cleaning the house for the open house I was having later that day. I washed the front windows and cleaned the front door with the hose. Later that day, before the open house, someone came to the door and I couldn't see out the peephole in the door, as it had fogged up from the water I used on the door. It was the FedEx man. I forgot I ordered materials for a class that had to be completed by the end of the month. When I opened the door, I was quite relieved. I couldn't get the fog cleaned out of the peephole, so I sat in the front by the window to allow me to see everyone before I opened the door. I was sure L might try to come to my open house and create a scene for me. The incident with L convinced me if I had any thought about staying in Walnut Creek, it was gone now. My son thought I should press charges, but I told him we knew the police were not going to be able to protect me. If I pressed charges I wasn't sure what reaction L would have, or what he would do. I felt sure I would sell my house and be gone by the end of summer. People were always looking for a house in this area because of the reputation of the schools.

Case Comes to WC: *July 1998*

I went to the airport in time to park and walk to the runway. It was our understanding that if I wasn't standing there when they departed from the plane to go to the baggage area and pick up their luggage and wait for me outside. He was a little surprised to see that I had made it on time. I told Case about L and not to open the door if he didn't know the person. There would be real estate agents showing the house, but they had a key and he didn't need to let them in. He wanted to go up to Mt. Diablo and take some pictures since this might be his last chance if I sold the house and moved out of the area. We had to check on mother before going to Lake Sequoia, as she had been placed in a new facility after her last visit to the hospital. I wanted to bring her television for her so she would have something to watch, but after I spent Saturday with her I knew she was not going to want to remain at the facility. There was a very disagreeable lady in the bed next to her who wanted to make sure that no one else came into her room, so she was as mean and horrible as she could be. She kept the air conditioning down to fifty degrees and if anyone touched the control she had a fit.

Case made the mistake of sitting on her bed when she was out of the room since there were no chairs available and when she returned she screamed at him, "Get off my bed."

Then mother made the mistake of picking up her glass by mistake to get a drink of water and the woman, who had been sitting outside the door watching us screamed, "Leave my things alone."

The doctor and nurse came into mother's room and wanted to conduct a psychological evaluation on her to see if she had any mental problems. They thought she was too demanding, and they wanted to know if there were any problems that could be helped with drugs for her anxiety. I thought it was amazing they would say that with what she had to put up with from her demanding roommate. Was this a chance for this facility to bill Medicare for more services?

After I left for Walnut Creek, mother called Bett and begged her to come and take her home, she couldn't stand being in there any longer. Bett could hear how desperate she was to get out of that place, and came to her rescue. The office tried to scare my daughter claiming she was taking full responsibility if anything happened to her.

When we were back in the Bay Area Case wanted to go to Alcatraz. I had a coupon for a brunch cruise around the bay. Since it was a Saturday afternoon the passengers were a mix of families, couples, and single people. We had a great brunch and the cruise was wonderful, with him taking lots of pictures. I also took the video camera and took as much footage of the bay that I could. That Sunday we went to Santa Cruz, to take more pictures and enjoy the beach. It was a cloudy, cold, overcast day so we didn't stay very long.

Brit decided not to come to California for the summer. I don't know why she didn't want to come. She wouldn't tell me what was going on, or why. It was unusual for her to miss the camping trip we did every summer. It was just Case, FJ and my grandson, and my two younger grandchildren. We always had a great time, but she was missed by all her friends who came at the same time every year, and especially the family.

September 30, 1998

I accepted an offer from another bank and they wanted me to come on board the first of the month so I would be their employee when the new bank took over on October 1st. That meant giving up the commissions I had pending. The bank manager couldn't understand why I wasn't giving two weeks notice. Usually the bank didn't want financial advisors to stay for the two weeks, and let them go immediately, even if they gave advance notice.

November 5, 1998

I listened to my messages when I came down to the kitchen in the morning. There was a message from L, he wanted me to turn over my home to him immediately. He didn't care if I went to the Walnut Creek Police, he was going to do whatever it took for him to get my house. I couldn't believe he would be so stupid to leave this message on my voicemail. I called the officer of the Walnut Creek Police and left him a message that I was going to proceed with my formal complaint against L. I'm glad that I didn't get that message the night before, as I would probably not have been able to sleep. I didn't want to think about going through the legal process and all that entailed.

November 6, 1998

I checked my messages early in the morning, but nothing from the officer and nothing from L. I called the Walnut Creek Police to check to see when the officer would be in, since I didn't have a copy of the police report and didn't want to start all over again explaining the story to someone else. He wasn't expected until after 9:30 p.m., so I would have to wait for a call from him.

November 9, 1998

After work, I decided it would be the time to stop by the Walnut Creek Police and file another complaint against L. The officer decided to file a separate account, since this was a threat in addition to the harassment. He said that the information would be sent to the District Attorney's office and it would then be the DA's decision if there was enough information to proceed. I called my voicemail and let him listen to the message L had left.

After the officer listened to the message he said, "The District Attorney is not going to like it when he hears L say, 'I don't care what you do with the Walnut Creek Police or the District Attorney. I want that house turned over to me.'"

The officer said he would bring L in and talk to him, and that would probably be enough to make him stop his threats. I don't really know how many years he had been calling me. I didn't know if he was the person puncturing tires of cars parked in front of my house for the past several years. I experienced too many for it to be considered an accident, and thought it was because I parked in the drug dealer's space in the city, a few blocks from where I worked.

~~~~~~~~~~~~~~~~

Sale of Home: *November 11, 1998*

I received an offer and the real estate contracts were signed by the buyers and the agent left my copy under the mat by the front door. By signing the contract, they acknowledged they were aware of the harassment problem with L and thought it would not be a problem for them.

I wanted to be mobile since I didn't know how secure my employment was going to be with the bank. I had already worked for three banks and they had all been bought out by another bank. The first bank I worked for I had a caller who asked if our bank was being bought out. I checked with the branch manager and she said no. A few days later, the new bank took over and it was utter chaos. I knew then to take rumors seriously when they concerned a bank.

There was to be a house inspection on Wednesday. The inspection was done and Thursday I received a call from the agent that the wife had some second thoughts about the problem with L and wasn't sure if she wanted to go ahead with the offer. I called my listing agent on Friday morning and told her to let other agents know that I would be accepting backup offers since there might be a problem, and she could call the selling agent for any further details.

I waited seventeen years to sell the house, but because of tax laws I needed to hold on to the house until I was fifty-five, so I could sell the house and not have to buy a more expensive house or pay capital gains taxes on the profit with limitations.

I received a call from the police officer who said he called L and left a message, but had not received a call from him so he was turning the case over to the District Attorney for a decision as to what would happen to L.

<hr />

November 22

Vi sent me an announcement about a position close to my family. I decided to send my application in order to keep all my options open. I had a telephone interview with them as I couldn't drive down for a person-to-person interview since they didn't give me advance notice. I didn't know if there was a private phone at the branch I was to be that day, so I might have to go to a pay phone in order to have the interview in privacy. I was not sure about accepting the position. It meant going back to a lower income, and I didn't know if I could do that.

<hr />

Thanksgiving

I wasn't sure how long mother's money was going to last, since it was costing about $1,400 a month to have someone come in the evening to care for her. One of the residents where mother lived said she goes into the hallway knocking on doors telling people she is hungry and doesn't have anything to eat. She had a refrigerator full of food from Meals on Wheels and a pantry stocked with canned goods, but she doesn't remember that. I think she gets lonely and wants companionship. Medicare sent a senior citizen out to visit with her, but they didn't have much to talk about so she thought it was a waste of her time.

Brit called while we were all at my sister's place celebrating Thanksgiving. I think she missed all of us and the fun we had when we were all together. There was always a lot of laughter and a lot of joking. I told her I hadn't been answering the phone because of the harassing calls I had been receiving. She didn't know about that, as I had not shared my problem with many people. She said she called me collect, but I never received the calls. The operator usually would let the phone ring until the call went through. If voicemail comes on, the operator disconnects the call. She said it worked when she called her dad. I had written her that I would use some of my miles to bring her out for Christmas and she could bring her friend if she wanted for company since I had to work.

I stayed with mother that night and she was very restless. Thanksgiving had been too much for her. I had a nightmare that she attacked me on the couch while I was sleeping. I don't know what brought that on, but I know several times she did not know who I was when I spent the night. I think she was very angry and frustrated about her limited physical abilities. After her stroke she was paralyzed on one side and had to wear a foot brace when she got up from bed. Mother continually commented that she didn't understand how our dad could still get around and even drove, but she was confined to her wheelchair. She felt that she took better care of her health than he had. The problem was, her doctors were overmedicating her and she continued to drink while she was taking her medications. I think that is what caused her stroke, and maybe that was why she was angry and frustrated. She realized she was partly responsible for her situation. I guess sometimes maybe she felt like pulling the covers over her head and not getting out of bed. I know things have been tough for her.

<hr />

December 1, 1998

I had another offer from a couple that saw the house. It was a ridiculous offer and I countered. Several days went by and I heard nothing and the time expired when they could respond. The agent called me and said she had another offer. I was busy and couldn't get home early and told her to leave the offer under my front doormat and I would read it. When I read it, the price was nowhere near what I wanted. I called the agent the next day and told her I would not be responding to the offer, and her buyers should not waste their time anymore and find another house that they could afford. She came back several days later and left a message saying she thought they finally realized what my bottom line was and that the house was being sold "as is." They were going to get estimates on some improvements and make me another offer.

~~~~~~~~~~~~~~~

December 14, 1998

I received a message from mother's nighttime aide that she had become uncontrollable, and she called the paramedics. Mother was in the hospital again. There was also a message from the hospital saying my mother was there and she was okay, but to call them. I knew there were going to be problems when I called mother the night before at 6:00 p.m. and she was just getting out of bed. I called her doctor several times previously and left messages that mother needed something to help her sleep at night and to decrease some of her medications because they were making her so anxious and unrestful. The doctor did not want to give her a sleep aid. I emphasized that if she went into a nursing home they would probably end up medicating her at night there. All I was asking for was some help so she could stay in her own home. The doctor said she would give her something very light and see how it worked. Her aide said mother had previously gotten up in the middle of the night, banging on the walls, and trying to get out of her apartment. Her aide tried to control her, but it was getting more and more difficult. Mother was in the kitchen boiling water for coffee and the aide wasn't sure, but she thought mother said she was going to throw the hot water at her. When I stayed with her over the Thanksgiving holiday I had a dream that she attacked me in my sleep and I couldn't defend myself because I was so groggy. My sister and I discussed what to do about mother, and we decided to keep mother's apartment during Christmas and probably start moving her out in January. I wanted to make sure that the nursing home she was in was going to be a good place for her. I was not looking forward to this, but knew it was time. We could no longer leave her alone and it was going to be difficult to find someone who would stay with her at night no matter how much we paid. The senior development where she lived did not want her to stay there any longer. The calls to 911 were disrupting the complex, and mother knocking on doors in her nightgown asking for food when she had food in her apartment were too numerous to ignore any longer.

I was concerned about the hospital where she was going to be admitted. My father had been in this hospital when he had an aneurysm in the abdomen. He received outstanding care in the Intensive Care Unit, but when he was moved out to his hospital room the care was different. His orderly tied him to a chair to get him to sit up daily. It was painful for him to sit up and my dad would crawl back in bed. Dad thought about filing a claim against the hospital, but the doctors had been so good to him, as he was considered their miracle patient. I told my dad when he was in the hospital that if the orderly looked into his eyes and saw my dad didn't like him it was going to be a difficult time for him. His life was in the orderly's hands now. He needed to practice and think love for the people who were taking care of him.

The Robbery

I was at the bank in Oakland, talking to the manager about the branch goals for investments, and went to the back to make a photocopy of my business plan for the branch. I was talking to one of the tellers as someone left us some chocolate éclairs as a gift. I told her I didn't usually eat sweets this early but couldn't resist the éclairs.

I just cut one in half and took a bite when she said, "Oh my God, we are being robbed."

I turned and looked at the monitor and there was a man with a sawed-off shotgun and a female accomplice. I could hear him shouting orders.

She asked me, "What should we do?"

I said, "Hide and pray."

We found a place in the supply closet and squatted down on the floor and prayed. I thought for sure he would come to the back where the vault was for more money. We could hear him shouting, "Hurry up. Get down on the floor. Get the money." While I was down on the floor I was thinking "is this the way my life is going to end?" I was warned by other employees if I worked long enough at the bank I was going to experience a robbery, but had been lucky so far. I wondered if my children and my family were going to read about me being killed in a bank holdup. Was this the way my life was going to end? We stayed on the floor for sometime until we thought it was over. No one came back for us. We finally stood up and looked at the monitor and saw the tellers moving around and decided it was safe to go out to the lobby. The police and FBI arrived and took statements from everyone. Since I hadn't been in the lobby when the robbery took place they didn't need a statement from me.

I asked the teller that was robbed, "What happened?"

She told me, "The female robber came to her and said, 'Give me all your money.'" She only gave her a $100 bill. The female robber looked at her and I am sure if she had a gun she would have shot the teller. She wanted more money and the teller gave her a few more bills, then the robber reached over and took money out of the drawer, it was then the teller said she set the silent alarm off.

I said, "Why did you do that? Don't you know if the police had shown up before the robbers left, we would have been trapped inside, and could have been shot? That man was desperate. You could tell by his voice and demeanor. It would have been best to let him leave and then set off the alarm."

I think she was looking to be a hero for the bank by keeping their money safe. I don't think she realized she could have been shot in the holdup and lost her life. I don't believe any compensation her family would receive from the bank would be enough to make up for their loss, but she was not thinking of that possibility.

The other teller did the same thing, only giving out small bills until the robber leaned over the counter and grabbed more of the money.

Another branch had been robbed and the teller wouldn't give the robber the money, and she had to testify at his trial. This was the incident that had given this teller the idea she had the option of not giving the money to a robber. She wanted to be a hero to the bank, but put our lives in danger. Any teller that did not give the money to a robber should have been fired. They put everyone's life in danger.

The other banks on the street had been robbed so many times they closed their branch. This was the first robbery for this bank. One of the security people from the bank said they would probably not be back since they didn't get much money, only four or five thousand dollars. I said that was a lot of money for them, they would be back.

The bank manager wanted to open back up at 3:00 p.m., but was given other orders. Everyone stayed in the branch and did busy work. We all talked about what went on. One of the customers saw the female robber walk in. When she realized what was going on, it was too late to warn us, as the robbery was taking place. After the robbery everyone said that while they were lying face down on the floor they had all been praying. We were sure that was the only thing that kept us safe and calm.

When I told Bett about the robbery, she said, "I bet you were praying weren't you?"

I said, "Absolutely, and so was everyone else."

The next day I was tired and didn't have the energy to make it to work, but decided it was probably best to keep busy.

After the robbery I started evaluating my goals and decided to take the position offered after my telephone interview, and move closer to mother so I could help her stay out of a nursing home.

December 17, 1998

The new position I accepted was going to mean a reduction in income, but I decided that I would be able to live comfortably on less. It would be a temporary appointment for four years, but I could apply for a permanent position if one became available. I would have retirement benefits and health benefits. It sounded good to me. No more working for commissions only. Maybe then I could save some more for my retirement, spend more time with my grandchildren, and help my daughter. I now had to make a decision when to tell my boss that I was taking a job to be closer to my mother.

Christmas: *1998*

Brit and Case came to stay with me for Christmas. I wasn't sure if Brit was going to come to California this Christmas, but I guess she must have missed seeing all of us. I checked the arrival times and realized that Case had given me two airlines for arrival. I called and left a message for them to call me and let me know which airline they were arriving on. I was at work when I listened to my voicemails and Case left a message.

I heard him say, "She isn't there," then he hung up.

He left no message about which airline they would be arriving on. I left work early to get to the airport and when I arrived I had time to kill so I sat in a hotel parking lot waiting for their plane. I decided it would be better to wait outside the terminal in my car, since I didn't know which airline and I would be able to see them or they would see me when they came out with their baggage. They knew if I was not at the gate to go to pick up their baggage, and I would be outside circling the airport since parking was not allowed for arrivals. I had gone around the airport four times and was on my fifth time and decided, well if they aren't there this time, there must be a problem. I was on the outside lane, not the lane to pick up passengers, when I saw Case's bright blue and red jacket. I honked and stood on my car door rim and hollered and waived to them. They came dragging their suitcases across the traffic and people behind me were honking waiting for me to move. I waited for others to make their pickup, now they would have to wait for me. Needless to say, I was not in a good mood.

I was stressed out and angry after waiting so long, and asked, "Didn't you receive my message? I didn't know which airline you were on."

Brit wanted to go shopping the next day before we left to see family. She wanted to buy gifts for her brother FJ, my grandson, and FJ's dad who always gave them gifts at Christmas. I told her to save her money, but this was what she wanted to do. We were going to have a five-dollar gift exchange on Christmas Eve so they both needed to shop for that gift. I bought some extra gifts for those who didn't have time to shop. Usually Bett didn't have time to shop and I didn't want them to be left out. We were going to have our celebration Christmas Eve and go skiing on Christmas Day.

Brit, Case and I went to mother's to sleep since she was in a nursing home again. She had called the paramedics again and they took her to the hospital. After she was checked out and they determined nothing was wrong with her they asked if she wanted to be discharged to a nursing home and she agreed. This particular home was not in a good area. I could tell by the address. I wanted to go that evening to see her, but my eyes are not good at night and since the neighborhood was not familiar to me I decided to go the next day.

We went to the nursing home and took her to lunch at a hotel downtown. I wanted a bright, cheery place and the hotel was the nicest place close to her nursing home. It was a nice, relaxing lunch. It was hard for her to sit a long period of time and she was eager to leave after lunch was over. She thought she was going back to her apartment, but I told her, "you have fired everyone, there is no one to take care of you, you'll have to wait until I can get someone to come back and take care of you."

We had a great time skiing on Christmas Day. I fixed sandwiches and took cookies to have with the hot chocolate we would buy at the ski resort. My grandchildren had a great time going down the hills on the snow tubes I bought them. When we drove back to Bett's house we finished up the leftovers and then it was time to drive back to mother's to spend the night. I had to get up early since I was going to the nursing home to pick up mother. The next morning when mother saw me, the first thing she said was, "Get me out of here." She was glad I was there to take her home. FJ and my grandson came by to see everyone before they left. Mother was starting to panic even before I left, and had called her friend twice within a few minutes to see when she would be coming to her apartment.

We had to drive back to Walnut Creek that night since I had to work on Monday. My granddaughter wanted to come home with us and spend more time with Brit and Case. Bett would drive to my house on New Year's Day to pick her up. I had to call a few people to see if I could find someone to watch her after Brit and Case left, as I had to work. We stopped in Walnut Creek to shop and had dinner before going home. Brit wanted to buy gifts for friends and family that she would be seeing after Christmas. When we went to bed Brit slept with me and my granddaughter slept at our foot in a sleeping bag. When I got up and left early she got in bed and slept next to Brit, just to be close to her. I left work early so we could go to San Francisco and have lunch and see the town. We parked close to Pier 39 and then took a bus to Union Square and had dinner at one of the diners. While we were waiting for a cable car to go back to Pier 39 a limo pulled up and said they were giving rides to Fisherman's Wharf for a reduced rate.

I said, "No, that is too much."

Brit said, "I'll pay"

So I said, "Okay then I'll pay half the costs."

We climbed into the limo with another lady and her daughter, it was so much fun, and we were having a great time. Case had brought his camera and was taking pictures of all the sights. This was my first limo ride that wasn't a funeral. The last time I rode in a limo was when my dad's wife died. We had a great time, and I didn't need any of the champagne they offered to have fun. FJ, my son, promised me a limo ride when I turned sixty, as he had done for his dad. I said I wanted my limo ride now, I might not make it to sixty, but I couldn't make him change his mind. When the limo arrived at Fisherman's Wharf it was hard to leave. I wanted it to go on forever. The next night we went to dinner and shopping in the mall. I told my granddaughter we don't usually have so much going on, doing something every evening, but this was a special time for all of us together and it was Christmas. I asked M from next door to watch my granddaughter, and Bett approved of him since she knew him and his mother would also be available. For New Year's Eve I picked up movies and my granddaughter and I had our own celebration with sparkling apple cider and lit some sparklers. The next day we watched the Rose Bowl parade until Bett and my grandson joined us.

I accepted an offer on the house and on January 1, 1999 I would be moving. Bett made a comment that she didn't know how I was going to get all my things packed. While she went shopping for bargains I watched my grandchildren outside playing and started packing. After eighteen years there was a great deal to move. I had garage sales at deep, deep discounts and gave away many things, not wanting to move anything I wouldn't be using.

The Move: *1999*

One thing about moving to a smaller city is the price of real estate is more affordable. I could afford my dream home. It was the home I thought about at night when I couldn't sleep. It was amazing how perfect it was. The backyard was like a park, but a park takes a lot of work. Brit did not want me to sell the house in Walnut Creek and said she wouldn't come and see me if I moved. She did come to my new home though and had many happy memories.

When I sold my house in Walnut Creek I moved hoping to be able to keep my mother out of a nursing home. I stayed with her in the evening and tried to get enough sleep to work during the day. Unfortunately, that didn't work out because she was up all night trying to leave the apartment thinking it was daytime. She often didn't recognize me when I was sleeping on her couch. I had to keep an eye open when she was up in case she decided I was the enemy. She threatened the last caretaker and sometimes had mistaken me for her since she had lost part of her eyesight due to her stroke.

When she went into the last nursing home I knew she would have to stay there. The facility had caring people working there, and since I came every day to visit her I believe she received better care. I even ate lunch with her at the home sometimes, as the food was very good. Other times we would go for a ride and get a hamburger at the local fast food places where they had a drive-up and we didn't have to get out of the car.

When she had her last stroke, it was horrible. I went to the hospital to see her, but I wasn't prepared for how bad it was going to be. I couldn't stop crying. I tried not to let her know I was crying so she wouldn't feel hopeless and know how bad it was. I stayed at the hospital with her for two days and then my sister came and stayed with her the third day while I went to work. It was good that I went back to work because then I knew that I had to get control of myself and stop crying. She couldn't talk and wasn't able to eat or drink. She had left a living will that she did not want to be resuscitated and didn't want tubes for feeding or water.

I had to make a decision for a hospice facility and instead of going to a new place; I chose the nursing home where she had been staying. The administrator assured me they had hospice care. When I went in to visit her she had been placed in a room with four other women. One woman was quite verbal and complained because mother kept throwing her covers off and her nightgown didn't always completely cover her. The next time I came in to visit her she was completely dressed and in the hallway with the other residents. I couldn't believe that they considered this hospice. The nurse in charge was giving directions to one of the caretakers regarding her care, and I saw the helper roll her eyes. I told the administrator I did not want someone who didn't like their job to be taking care of my mother. I was ready to take her to a new facility. This was causing me a great deal of stress to come in each time and have to go over her care. I thought this was going to cause me to have a stroke. This was not my idea of hospice. The reason I had her brought back there was because most of the caretakers knew her and cared about her.

Finally, they gave her a private room where family could sit with her in her last hours. My sister came to the home and we sat with her. When the home called me and said she "passed" in the middle of the night I went to visit one last time before they took her away. We had a family memorial service at my home and the pastor came and officiated. The plan was to take her ashes back to Virginia for burial July 1st when her family would be coming back to visit.

Shortly after that my dad moved into an apartment after he was evicted from the house he had lived in and maintained for over thirty years. He had fallen outside the building and when an ambulance was called he refused to go to the hospital. The police said they could not make him go if he didn't want to. He suffered for two weeks with the pain, he was lucky he had his friend Bd helping him as much as possible. When he finally agreed to go to the VA hospital he had a broken arm and three ribs that had punctured his lung. I had just seen him that weekend and I was at work when I received an email from my daughter that "granddad died." I couldn't believe she would send an email to work instead of calling. We had another family service at my home with the pastor and my sister and I were going to take his ashes back at the same time as my mother. I wanted to bury him with my mother at her family's cemetery, but since he said he wanted to be buried with the veterans, we took his ashes to Arlington National Cemetery. It was a beautiful service and one that many veterans' families don't take advantage of.

After the service for my mother I asked my cousin to reserve a spot for me beside mother. Since I wasn't sure the space would always be there, as the markers would be moved when the lawn was cut, I asked him to buy me a headstone just like my mother's and I sent him the money. Now when I pass away all my children have to do is to ship my ashes back to one of my cousins and they will do the rest. My sister

Prip still does not have a headstone. She is buried with her son R, but because of technicalities involving unions and moving the headstone we have not been able to make the change. We looked into buying a headstone, but somehow it didn't happen. This is one thing my children won't have to worry about.

~~~~~~~~~

Happy Ending: *2006*

My grandson wanted to know when I was going to finish my book. I told him when I could give it a happy ending. The best news I had was that my niece who had been given up for adoption was able to find us. I thought I was going to have to write to Oprah to help us find her. We weren't able to find any information on the adoption. I always felt she had been adopted by an Armenian family since her dad was Armenian. Many times, when I saw a young girl I thought resembled my sister or my niece, I would ask her where she was born and what her birthdate was. It was unexpected when I received an email from my daughter that my niece R had found us, and she lived in my area. I didn't have any other information except she was in real estate and her last name. I went on the internet and tried to find her, but wasn't sure of the spelling of her name. I waited for a call, but didn't receive one, so I called and left messages for all of them. I couldn't believe that we had been looking for her for over twenty years and I couldn't get her telephone number. It was two weeks before I received her telephone number. I immediately called R and invited her and her family to dinner. She was married and had a daughter and was pregnant with a second child. Since it was Easter, my daughter and grandchildren would be visiting when R and her family came to dinner. It was amazing to see her and think of all the years we had lost by not being a part of her life. She said all her life she had wanted to find her mother. She knew from an early age that she was adopted, as was her brother, by an Armenian couple. She said the only way she found us was someone had a computer program that allowed her to look up her original birth certificate. She was then able to find Nk, her biological sister. At first, she drove by Nk's apartment to see what she looked like. She still wasn't sure they were related because Nk was dark and looked like her Armenian father, and R was fair like our side of the family.

R finally was able to get up the courage to call and asked her, "Is your mother's name Prip?"

My niece said, "Yes, what is this about?"

She said, "Prip is my birth mother."

My niece said, "Oh." She knew this was her birth sister.

R wasn't aware that Prip had been deceased for twenty years from cancer. The sisters met and talked about how their lives were so different. I was right when I thought she had been adopted by an Armenian couple and was raised in their community. Nk visited with her father's other children, but didn't seem to find a place to fit into their lives. There was no animosity from her father's family. Their goal had been to be better parents to their children.

It was hard for R to understand why her mother had given her up for adoption, but then became pregnant again by the same father and decided to keep that baby.

The only thing I could say was that I was sure Prip suffered every day after she gave her up for adoption. I think it was the postpartum depression she was going through, and if she had financial and physical support she would not have made the same decision. She was always a jovial, happy person, but in this instance, she wasn't able to get back to her old happy self. I told her I knew after giving her up there was a hole in her heart and she could not go through that again with the second pregnancy. Living with our dad made it more difficult for her to have a positive outlook. I lived with him and his wife for a few months when I came to California while I was waiting for my house to be built. The only way we were able to live with them was to stay out until dark by going to the park or other events in the area. We didn't eat there because the kitchen and rest of the house was filthy. It was hard to take a bath in their bathroom since it never was cleaned either. I know when she was living with our dad and his wife how difficult it must have been for her taking care of a baby. After giving birth, coming back to that atmosphere was very depressing for her. She must have given up hope that there was any other option. There did not seem to be any other way. It is hard for someone who hasn't been in that situation to understand. She told everyone that the baby died, not that she had given her up for adoption. That was the only way she knew how to deal with her decision so she wouldn't have to talk about what happened and why.

I always thought one of the reasons my sister developed cancer had to do with giving up her baby for adoption and then her son was hit by a car and died. She lost two children and died from a broken heart, as well as from the chemo-therapy and radiation treatment for the cancer. I have tried to relay what a difficult time she had from the time she was three years old when she was not with our mother, and how that experience stayed with her for her entire life. I know she loved her children very much, and is looking down on both of them smiling, happy to see the lives they are living. Our sister was a very loving person.

~~~~~~~~~~~~

Ending

A therapist I was seeing after the separation in Walnut Creek said that my life was like a soap opera. I had some unique challenges, but others have had worse things happen. I always wondered if God was testing me. Was I being tested to be an example for my children?—so they would know that no matter what happens in life, you have to pick yourself up and keep on going. I sometimes felt I was like the Energizer Bunny, and could never quit no matter what. I stopped seeing one therapist when she made a comment at one session that it had been six months since Greg left and I should be over our divorce. At the time my son was just barely seven months old so I knew a lot of what I was going through was postpartum depression. I was not taking any drugs but trying to use exercise and meditation to help my moods, and not give up. I wonder how she would have handled the same situation.

For most of my challenges I knew there must be a solution. My strategy was: if plan A doesn't work, go to plan B, or plan C until I can find the answer. I have tried not to blame my mother or my father for not always being there for us. I know they did not have an easy life growing up, and their parents didn't have any self-help books or Dr. Spock.

After I was married my mother and I became best friends, and she was my therapist, as she was someone that I could tell anything to without her being judgmental. After she passed away I lost my trusted therapist. There was no one I could call and tell all my woes to like her. I only wish that all of my children and I had the same relationship. I hope by writing this book they will be able to understand decisions that were made that affected their lives, and some of the questions they may have. I waited too long to ask my mother many questions, because she could not remember those instances by then. Like most seniors who have health problems we never know when the end will come. My cousin asked me not long ago, "How's your health?"

I told him, "It's like the drip, drip, drip of a faucet. I'm waiting for the Big Bang to happen that will end it all." That's why I feel a sense of urgency in writing this book.

I asked my dad what his mother died from and he said a broken heart. I know she cared for my cousin and I and then when the war was over, she was no longer needed. No one was able to find a space for her in their home. I remember my dad and mother looking for a bigger apartment, but never made the move. Maybe money was a factor. I think my dad's behavior would have been different if our grandmother lived with us, as he loved her very much and would not want to disappoint her. She died shortly after she made the move to Ohio. That must have been the reason he said she died from a broken heart. I wonder how many women who lost their children to death and court issues, or have been in a marriage for over forty years and are left to start over, recover from their broken heart.

I believe I have been blessed to have been able to accomplish many of my dreams and not dwell on the disappointments. I read something that I considered good advice, "The best revenge is to lead a good life." I could have made some disastrous decisions that would have affected my children and family negatively, but tried to think of them instead. The right thing to do is sometimes more difficult.

I took Brit and Case to see the movie *Perfect Storm* and after viewing it, I told them I considered taking them and sailing around the world with a friend. I know we probably wouldn't have made it very far before the Coast Guard would have put an end to the trip, and it would have caused legal problems.

I was able to make the trip to Brit's graduation and stayed with a friend of her's close by her dad's house. We had a nice time just cuddling on the couch and enjoying our time together. I think she really must have missed me. We made deviled eggs for the get-together after the graduation. Then we drove to Delaware to visit my aunt who arranged a family party with cake and gifts for Brit. She had seen Brit when she was a baby when her dad and I drove to see them. It was so nice to see everyone since this was the first time some members had seen my two younger children.

At Case's graduation, my older son and grandson, sister and her mate were able to make it to the event. There was a get-together at their dad's house that we all attended. Later we drove to Ocean City for a family get-together and even met up with a roommate from Walnut Creek. I went to his college graduation with my friend Vi. I asked him to make reservations at a restaurant where we could all have lunch together so he wouldn't have to choose which family he was going to celebrate with. My good friend Jo came with her spouse and three sons, and afterwards we were able to walk around and enjoy the park-like atmosphere. He skipped the ceremony for his master's degree. He told me I could come to his next graduation.

Brit graduated from college and started working on her master's degree. She changed majors when she decided that being a social worker was too depressing for her. When she told me what her major was I didn't say anything. I think it caused her to recall too many memories of what she and her brother went through due to divorce. I wasn't surprised when she changed her major to English. Maybe she will write her own book.

I know we didn't have the time together during summer and Christmas for me to be a mother to them. The test will come if they choose to stay in contact with me and we are able to spend time together now that they are in charge of their visits and telephone calls.